Cybernetics for the Social Sciences

Sociocybernetics and Complexity

Volumes published in this Brill Research Perspective are listed at *brill.com/rpsc*

Cybernetics for the Social Sciences

By

Bernard Scott

BRILL

LEIDEN | BOSTON

This paperback book edition is simultaneously published as issue 1.2 (2020) of *Sociocybernetics and Complexity*, DOI:10.1163/25900587-12340002.

Library of Congress Control Number: 2021903844

Typeface for the Latin, Greek, and Cyrillic scripts: "Brill". See and download: brill.com/brill-typeface.

ISBN 978-90-04-46434-6 (paperback)
ISBN 978-90-04-46449-0 (e-book)

This book is printed on acid-free paper and produced in a sustainable manner.

Contents

Cybernetics for the Social Sciences

Bernard Scott
Independent Scholar
bernces1@gmail.com

Abstract

This publication meets a long-felt need to show the relevance of cybernetics for the social sciences (including psychology, sociology, and anthropology). User-friendly descriptions of the core concepts of cybernetics are provided, with examples of how they can be used in the social sciences. It is explained how cybernetics functions as a transdiscipline that unifies other disciplines and a metadiscipline that provides insights about how other disciplines function. An account of how cybernetics emerged as a distinct field is provided, following interdisciplinary meetings in the 1940s, convened to explore feedback and circular causality in biological and social systems. How encountering cybernetics transformed the author's thinking and his understanding of life in general, is also recounted.

Keywords

Cybernetics – social sciences – first order cybernetics – second order cybernetics – transdiscipline – metadiscipline

•••

> My purpose is to bring to awareness much that is taken for granted. By this means, I hope to increase self-identity, intensify experience and decrease alienation. In a word, to take a small step along the road of self-knowledge to help reintroduce man to himself.
>
> EDWARD T. HALL, *The Hidden Dimension* (1969, p. x)

∴

 | DOI:10.1163/9789004464490_002

Prolegomena

In the beginning, the Lord said, "Let there be light" and there was light.
In the beginning, Heinz von Foerster said, "Let there be sight" and there was light.
The physicist said, "In the beginning, there was the big bang."
The cybernetician said, "Tell me a story that explains how it is that you can tell me a story about the big bang or, come to that, how it is that you can tell me a story at all."

"The force that through the green fuse drives the flower
Drives my green age; that *blasts* the roots of trees
Is my destroyer."

DYLAN THOMAS

∴

Dear reader, we begin with two human observers, you and me. We are having an imaginary conversation. I imagine you imagining me imagining you imagining me.... You imagine me imagining you imagining me imagining you.... In principle, these repetitions of forms embedded in forms could go on to infinity. They are examples of *recursion* (writing again), also known as the *re-entry* of a form into a form. They are also examples of self-reference (reflexivity), as can be clearly seen in the form, "I imagine me imagining me imagining me imagining me ..."

I imagine is a process; the *me's* and *you's* I am imagining are the products of that process.

However, in our ordinary experience of thinking, we do not generate (or *compute*) an infinity of forms. Why is this? The simplest answer is that we run out of the energy available for thinking. By the time the energy is replenished, our thought has terminated and needs to be reconstructed. There is only so far that we can get when we imagine imaginings or construct perspectives of perspectives (meta-perspectives). Our thought processes are *embodied.* They do not exist separate from the brain/body system. There are limits on how much thinking can be done at any one time. As well as energetic limits, there are capacity limits, depending on the speed of processing in the brain and the size of what psychologists refer to as 'working memory' (roughly equivalent to the surface area of an individual's cerebrum).

What does it mean to be embodied? To answer, I will begin my story with the big bang. (I could, of course choose some other myth as my starting point. I choose this one because it is a familiar idea in the culture in which I find myself.)

The big bang releases energy/matter: there are processes with products. There are events with *duration in time* and entities with *extension in space*. The physicist, in his theorising (Greek, *theoria*, picture), says that, from an initial state of symmetry (balance, equilibrium, stability), the big bang breaks the symmetry and the laws of physics emerge. Without these laws (constraints), the energy/matter released would instantly dissipate. There would be no time. There would be no observers. The source from which everything comes would be the same as the sink to which everything goes.

In the physicist's theory, the emergence of the cosmos (a universe displaying order) conforms to the laws of thermodynamics (Greek, *thermo dynamis*, heat power). The first law states that energy/matter cannot be created or destroyed. The second law states that disorder or 'entropy' (Greek, *en trope*, turning into) in the universe is always increasing. The arrow of time is irreversible. The final end is envisaged as a time when entropy/disorder has reached its maximum. (This is also known as the 'heat death' of the universe.)

The flow of energy/matter from the source (the big bang) to the sink (maximum disorder, heat death) can be likened to the flowing of a stream. The emerging lawfulness is like the rocks and irregularities in the stream bed that affect the flow of the water and cause eddies and whirlpools to form. These eddies and whirlpools are islands of order that, as they come into being, temporarily reverse the second law of thermodynamics and reproduce themselves as stable organisations: galaxies, stars, planets, living systems, human observers. For us humans, our local star, the sun, is the major energy source that drives and maintains the biosphere (Greek, *bios sphaira*, life sphere). The biosphere is a dynamic system that circulates matter in various forms, providing ecosystems for all life (Greek, *oikos systema*, home system). It is intimately connected to the dynamics of our planet, as the oceans, the atmosphere, the earth's crust, mantle and core interact.

The physicist sees himself as the observer of an objective reality that is external to himself. In contrast, the cybernetician is part of his theory; he explains himself to himself as a system of thoughts – a narrative – that reproduces itself as a stable but ever-changing self-conscious self, embodied in a brain/body system that constantly reproduces and renews itself. Just as thoughts are embodied, so are our bodily reactions experienced as feelings and emotions (affect) and interpreted (old English, *felan*, to touch, to experience; Latin, *ex movere*, *emovere*, out move; *ad factus*, *affectus*, to done).

Whereas the physicist believes that he is discovering reality, the cybernetician knows he is constructing a reality. In the objective reality of the physicist armed with scales, a ruler and a clock, a universal law has been discovered that shows the equivalence of energy (E) and matter (m): $E = mc^2$, where *c*, the speed of light, is a constant for all observers, even though their reference frames may be accelerating relative to each other. In the invented realities of cyberneticians, when observers converse, they, to some extent at least, share a reality; they synchronise; they coordinate. When this happens, the rate of change of change is the same for those observers. Their clocks are ticking at the same rate; their rulers and scales make similar measurements. For a while, at least, you and I are in synchrony, as reader and imagined narrator.

Part 1 About This Publication and a First Look at Cybernetics

1 *The Aim*

This first part is introductory. It provides a first look at cybernetics and describes how the book is structured. I have been thinking and writing about cybernetics for some 50 years. All through that time, I have seen the need for a text that communicates the main ideas of cybernetics in a user-friendly way, avoiding the formalisms of logic and mathematics that are off-putting for many readers, but still providing the sense that cybernetics is, within the limits that it itself prescribes, a coherent discipline. Many of my fellow cyberneticians have voiced the same need, saying that what is required is a text or academic course concerned with 'Cybernetics 101', to use the American style of referring to introductory undergraduate programmes. One reason I believe that this has not yet been satisfactorily achieved is that no two cyberneticians see the discipline in quite the same way. Another reason, I suggest, is that one course suitable for all undergraduates, whatever their speciality, is asking too much. Specialists in physics, biology, psychology, sociology and their subdisciplines have different interests, different learning styles and different ways of looking at the world. In constructing this publication, my eye has been mainly on the social sciences. There is much that I write about that may be of interest to students of other disciplines but there is likely to be much that is not. However, the publication should be of interest to anyone wishing to gain a broad understanding of the human condition and the world in which she finds herself.

Many years ago, in a seminal essay entitled, "The architectural relevance of cybernetics", the cybernetician, Gordon Pask, single-handedly brought about a pedagogic and practical revolution in architecture and the broader field of design (Pask, 1969b). In that paper, Pask explains why, after an initial enthusiastic uptake, the formal and technical disciplines, such as engineering, physics, chemistry, and large parts of biology and experimental psychology, seemed to lose interest in cybernetics. Pask believes this is because those disciplines had existing paradigms (theoretical and empirical) for developing their disciplines. They took what they thought of interest from cybernetics and carried on as usual with their specialist concerns. In contrast, the disciplines of architecture and design studies lacked agreed paradigms. Pask offered cybernetics as a way of making up for this deficit. His proposal was taken up enthusiastically. Interests in cybernetics developed that have proved to be fruitful and enduring.

In the social sciences, the story has been more varied. Cybernetics played a large part in the development of cognitive psychology. Cybernetics and what are now known as the systems sciences helped transform organisational psychology and management science. However, in the social sciences (social psychology, sociology, anthropology, political science, and economics), the impact of cybernetics has been more varied and less coherent. There have been several leading lights (for example, Talcott Parsons, Walter Buckley) who have explicitly used cybernetic ideas and also, from an early stage, a group of enthusiasts emerged who wished to bring cybernetics and systems thinking ideas into the disciplines in which they worked. It was in this context that the terms 'social cybernetics' and 'sociocybernetics' came into use. The former term tends to be used in the English-speaking world; the latter term is more commonly used in the non-English-speaking world. I have had long-standing connections with the international sociocybernetics community and for that reason I use the term in this publication where the context is obviously social. In other cases, I use the term 'cybernetics' to emphasise the role that cybernetics plays as a coherent, unifying transdiscipline and metadiscipline.[1]

2 *What Is Cybernetics?*

Let us begin with a first attempt at understanding what cybernetics is about. The person who coined the name, Norbert Wiener, wrote a book with the title *Cybernetics or Control and Communication in the Animal and the Machine* (Wiener, 1948). He took the term 'cybernetics' from the Greek word 'kubernetes', meaning 'steering', 'steersman', and 'steersmanship'. I will take the terms control and communication in turn and see how Wiener's definition can be elaborated. Later in the publication, I look at the key concepts of cybernetics in more detail. My aim here is to provide some 'advance organisers', messages that prepare the ground.

---

1 For an explanation of how I am using these terms, see part 6.

'Control' refers to the idea that in a complex system one part may have a determining effect on how another part (or parts) behaves. As examples, in the system 'classroom', a teacher may control – or attempt to control – the students; in a central heating system, a thermostat may control the temperature of the building; in the system 'steam engine', a 'governor' may put limits on the rate at which a machine operates. Another kind of 'governor' (a boss) may control a political state, a business or a public institution. In a 'living system', genes exert control on how the system develops and operates. A person, a 'social actor', may, within limits, control how he or she behaves in a particular context. The limits (also referred to as 'constraints') may be physical – humans cannot fly unaided – or social: constraints imposed by rules, laws, norms. Synonyms of 'control' include 'manage', 'steer', 'govern', 'facilitate'.

Let us now move on to the second of Wiener's terms, 'communication'. To highlight how important and ubiquitous is communication, note that for any controller to work effectively it must be able to communicate with the parts or subsystems that it is trying to control. In brief, it needs to be able to send messages informing the subsystems of changes they should make and it needs to receive messages from subsystems informing the controller of the subsystems' current states with respect to the controller's 'aims' or 'goals' (the terms are used here as synonyms). The goals may be very varied: to hit a particular target or to construct, maintain, recall, recognise or destroy a state of affairs of some sort. Here are a few examples: hitting a bull's-eye with an arrow, riding a bicycle without falling off, negotiating an agreement, maintaining harmony in a social group, maintaining the parameters of physiological processes within desired limits. The messages from the controlled to the controller are usually referred to as 'feedback' or 'knowledge of results'. A message that communicates information about how far the current state of affairs deviates from the desired state of affairs is referred to as 'negative feedback', as it denotes an error or difference that needs to be eliminated or minimised. A steersman looks to see how accurately his vessel is aiming towards his desired destination. If the messages fed back to him indicate deviation, he makes corrections accordingly, to minimise the deviation. The term 'positive feedback' is used to refer to messages which have the effect of increasing or amplifying a deviation from some set value. Examples of this latter are chain reactions in explosions, increases in population as successful breeding occurs and the spread of rumours or diseases throughout a community.

We now have a sight of what cybernetics is about: it abstracts similarities of form from a wide variety of systems to highlight the structures and processes that they have in common. It is primarily interested in a system's organisation, not what it is made of (it's 'fabric').

Having recognised at a high level of abstraction the form 'controller and controlled and the communication between them', we can now highlight a particular aspect of that form, its 'circularity' or, equivalently, its 'circular causality' (the term is used in contrast to the terms 'one way' or 'linear causality'). The controller affects the controlled and feedback from the controlled affects the controller in a circular process or loop. It is this circularity in how systems and parts of systems communicate that gives cybernetics its peculiar and universal significance. Circular causality is ubiquitous in complex systems at all scales, from the smallest to the cosmic. As my friend, Ranulph Glanville, liked to say, "Cybernetics is the discipline that takes circularity seriously."

Let us now look at the other two of Wiener's terms, 'animal' and 'machine'. In brief, it is generally agreed from the broad span of Wiener's interests that by animal he is referring to any system that partakes of the biological or social and by machine he is referring to any system that is an artefact of human devising. Under his term 'animal', we can include all systems that are usually distinguished as 'living' (plants, animals) or 'natural' (oceans, forests, ecosystems in general). Under the term 'machine', we can include mechanical devices, power plants, and all forms of information technology from computers to flags and 'talking drums'. We can also distinguish hybrid systems, understood as some combination of the 'animal and machine', for example, a horse and cart, a zoo, and all systems that are typically distinguished as 'social' (families, business organisations, societies, cultures).

It is worth emphasising now - and this is a point that we will return to later – in cybernetics, all the different systems that are distinguished are distinguished by a human observer. Communities of observers may agree about the distinctions made. They may also disagree. In their conversations, observers strive to reach consensus. They use reasoned argument (logic) and evidence to explain and justify their points of view. They may or may not understand each other's points of view (perspectives). They may or may not agree about how well they understand each other. Given that there are understandings of each other's understandings, there may or may not be agreement about the matter at hand. As a matter of choice, further investigations and further conversations may or may not be pursued. There may be an agreement to disagree. Conversations in everyday life may approximate the form of scientific conversations more or less closely. To capture this overall state of affairs concerning the conversations of human observers, I have formulated five "Laws of Observation and Action". They are:

1. There is always a bigger picture.
2. There is always another level of detail.
3. There is always another perspective.
4. There is always error.

5. There is always the unexpected.

I have been well aware of these laws as I have been writing this publication.

3 *How the Publication Is Structured*

As per the contents listing, this publication consists of a set of relatively short parts, divided into sections. Once the reader has some familiarity with what cybernetics is about, the parts can be consulted in any order. However, if the reader is new to cybernetics, I suggest that, after this part, she next reads parts 2, 3 and 4. There is a certain amount of unavoidable repetition as the concepts of cybernetics are deployed in different contexts. I have used cross-referencing to make this clear and to minimise the repetition. Since the publication is intended to be a scholarly text, I have provided references and footnotes.

Part 2 is largely autobiographical. My thinking is that an account of my journey towards being a cybernetician may give the reader an early sense of what cybernetics offers, personally as well as professionally.

Part 3 is a more straightforward account of cybernetics and how it came to be. Although it goes into much more detail than is provided in parts 1 and 2, it is still a relatively brief account of the discipline and its history. I provide references to other sources and there is more fleshing out in later parts.

Part 4 provides some technical 'meat' for the publication. In it, there is a selection of what I see as the core set of concepts that give cybernetics its shape and coherence. For each of the concepts, there is a definition and some commentary. This material could have gone into an appendix. However, I decided to insert it in the main text of the publication to bring it more strongly to the attention of the reader. She may well find it helpful, having read the part, to refer back to it for clarifications when reading other parts.

As is to be expected, the concepts are related one to another and are defined in terms of each other (they 'entail' each other). They have the form of a network with circular connections (the cybernetician, Gordon Pask, refers to this form as a concept 'mesh'). This reflects the circular processes by which a coherent set of concepts give rise to each other in thought as a stable (memorable, reproducible) whole. Ranulph Glanville, and I were collaborating on constructing the concept mesh found in part 4 at the time of his death. I have done my best to complete the project without him.

Part 5 discusses what we mean by the term 'messages'. I distinguish between the mechanical transmission of signals, using a code of some kind, and human conversations, where the meaning (the semantics) of a message is interpreted by the receiver. There is a discussion of what it means to say that participants in a conversation understand each other and come to agree, disagree or agree to disagree. To anticipate, and as an example, although there may be syntactic rules about how to combine words, and semantic rules (as in a lexicon or dictionary) about how words should be interpreted, the interpretation of a sentence will depend on how the receiver views the context: the 'pragmatics' (practicalities) of the situation. For example, this sentence, "Baby swallows fly", has two possible interpretations.

Part 6 takes a broad look at the ways that cybernetics, acting as a transdiscipline and a metadiscipline, can help to integrate human knowledge holistically and coherently, albeit, in an open-ended way. My purpose here is to emphasise just how powerful and useful cybernetics is as a unifying perspective. It provides relatively clear and simple ways of understanding the world and the human condition. This is a theme I emphasise repeatedly throughout the publication. Cybernetics, used reflexively (thinking about one's own thinking and acting) and pedagogically (helping others think about their thinking and acting), has the power to liberate humans from their 'mental chains', conceptual confusions and harmful practices.

In Part 7, I say more about how cybernetics can be employed as an intellectual tool and as an aid for effective communication. I defend the thesis that cybernetics should not be adulterated by alien paradigms such as Freudian psychology or phenomenology.

Part 8 addresses the discipline of psychology, in particular, the vexed topic of 'consciousness', which continues to have vast numbers of intellectuals and innocent bystanders in the grip of conceptual confusion. As part of the discussion, I provide an extended account of human learning and the associated activities of perceiving, acting, remembering and feeling as a unified system.

In Part 9, I briefly discuss the concept of a 'social network'. I provide a conceptual overview of the topic. As an example, I ask, "What is the difference, if any, between a social network and a social system?" I do not attempt to summarise the broader literature in which the term is been used.

In Part 10, I discuss how sociocybernetics can help us understand possible world futures. Here, cybernetics is explicitly used as a transdiscipline that can bring order to interdisciplinary research. I briefly mention some empirical studies but these are just a few selections from a vast array of relevant data and speculative theorising. My main aim is to offer some conceptual clarification that can help bring some order to the vast and varied fields of study (many of which are very specialised) relevant for understanding possible world futures. In particular, I discuss what it means to be 'holistic' in our concerns.

In Part 11, I discuss sociocybernetic understandings of cultural transmissions and transformations. Again, the main aim is to provide some conceptual clarification. I argue that we cannot globally move towards the futures we desire concerning a healthy ecosystem if we do not also make inroads into the vexing problems of the conflicts and misunderstandings that undermine attempts to work cooperatively. To change a society for the better, we need to develop understandings about how it works.

In Part 12, I provide a brief summary of what I have attempted to do in this publication. I also give links to resources for the reader who wishes to look more deeply into cybernetics. I then give myself the freedom to make some exhortations about how we should think and act, collectively and wisely. In the final section, I look a little more closely at how, as individuals, we live our lives: our values, attitudes, and ethics.

Part 2 A Life in Cybernetics

1 *Encountering Cybernetics*

Between 1964 and 1968, I was an undergraduate at Brunel University, studying psychology. I was on a 'sandwich course', meaning that periods of study were interspersed with work placements. In my first two years of study, I accrued very mixed feelings about psychology as a scientific discipline. Only the behaviourists claimed to be fully scientific. The rest of the discipline appeared to be a ragbag of disparate topics, studied and theorised about in a wide variety of ways. The curriculum consisted of courses of lectures on largely unrelated topics: learning theory, perception, social psychology, individual differences, psychopathology, organisational psychology, and developmental psychology. The curriculum also included some lectures on biology, sociology and social anthropology, taught as separate subjects. There was an early superficial mention of cybernetics in Robert Borger's lectures on learning theory but nothing substantial was covered. I was an indifferent and poorly motivated student in the midst of what I saw as a mess of a discipline, in which my teachers, espousing different paradigms, were incapable of constructive conversations with one another. It was cybernetics that eventually enabled me to make sense of this mess and inspired me to become an enthusiastic scholar.

In 1966, I had the good fortune to attend a course of lectures on cybernetics given by David Stewart, a newly appointed lecturer in the Department of Psychology.[2] I had previously read W. Grey Walter's (1963) *The Living Brain* and Wladyslaw Sluckin's (1954) *Minds and Machines*. Both helped me appreciate the larger philosophical tradition in which problems of mind and body, freewill and determinism have been debated. I recall that Sluckin reported on

2 David continues to be active and, as I write, is the vice-president of the UK's Cybernetics Society.

developments in cybernetics and related disciplines but was not committed to cybernetics as a unifying transdiscipline. David Stewart's stimulating presentations helped me be aware of that possibility. I was attracted to the thesis that cybernetics is a transdiscipline, one that brings together other disciplines in a unifying and enlightening way. It made sense that there should be unity in diversity. It made sense that there should be a discipline as important and as general as physics but which was complementary to it. I grasped this as the aphorism "Physics is about matter and energy; cybernetics is about control and communication."

I began to see how cybernetic concepts could provide explanations of psychological processes in far more sophisticated ways than those offered by the behaviourists. Thanks to David Stewart, I had the opportunity to work with the cybernetician, Gordon Pask (1928–1996). At that time, Pask was Research Director of System Research Ltd., an independent, non-profit research organisation in Richmond, Surrey, UK. I had a six months' work placement there as a research assistant. Pask was the most obviously intellectually brilliant person I have ever met. I was awed just to be in his presence. I obtained a preprint of Pask's most recent paper and studied it in detail (Pask, 1966). To make sense of it, I spent many hours looking up the references and reading Pask's earlier papers. From this reading, I gained what had eluded me thus far: an overarching, satisfying conceptual framework that allowed me to make sense of the biological, the psychological and the social in a coherent and enlightening way. I was becoming a cybernetician.

2 *Becoming a Cybernetician*

Eventually, I read W. Ross Ashby's (1956) *Introduction to Cybernetics*. I think all of us who love cybernetics have drawn inspiration from Ashby's bold declaration that "The truths of cybernetics are not conditional on their being derived from some other branch of science. Cybernetics has its own foundations" (p. 1). He goes on, "Cybernetics ...... takes as its subject-matter the domain of 'all possible machines'" (p. 2). This is followed by "Cybernetics, might, in fact, be defined as the study of systems that are open to energy but closed to information and control – systems that are 'information-tight'" (p. 4).[3] Here Ashby is reflecting cybernetics' primary concern with circular causality and anticipating later emphases on 'organisational closure' (see next part). Ashby's development of his ideas is underpinned by his use of diagrams and mathematics. He takes great pains to make their use accessible and transparent.

3 Ashby uses the terms 'machine' and 'system' as synonyms. Both terms refer to 'things that persist'.

Ashby highlights two primary uses of cybernetics: "It offers a single vocabulary and a single set of concepts for representing the most diverse types of systems" and "It offers a method for the scientific treatment of the system in which complexity is outstanding and too important to be ignored" (pp. 4–5). There are perhaps those who would disagree with Ashby's claim that cybernetics provides "a single vocabulary and a single set of concepts", pointing to the proliferation of specialist vocabularies and conceptual schema within the cybernetics and 'systems thinking' areas. However, I suggest that in this variety, there is much consensus and that there is an underlying structure of primary concepts that makes cybernetics what it is, much of which is captured in Ashby's formal approach. In 1995, I attended an international multidisciplinary conference, entitled *Einstein meets Magritte,* and witnessed much difficulty, even distress, as physicists, philosophers, artists, and humanities specialists attempted to communicate with each other about a range of issues, many of global concern. Within the larger conference, there was a symposium, convened by Francis Heylighen, on *The Evolution of Complexity*, with fifty or so participants, including management scientists, biologists, systems scientists, psychologists, neuroscientists, sociologists, engineers, computer scientists, and physicists. The remarkable thing about this symposium, in contrast to the main conference, was that there was much effective interdisciplinary communication. This was because all the participants did have some grounding in concepts to do with complex systems and cybernetics. Indeed, many of the participants drew directly on Ashby, himself. Thus, was the master vindicated.

Further reading persuaded me not only of the value of cybernetics as a unifying transdiscipline but also that cyberneticians were not naive or trivial in their epistemologies, their understandings of how we know and what may be known, and that there was a deep sense of metadisciplinary self-awareness in their shared enterprise, that cybernetics, as a discipline that studies other disciplines (a metadiscipline), is also a discipline that studies itself. I learned that there was an informal collegiate that included, amongst others, Gregory Bateson, Warren McCulloch, Heinz von Foerster, Gordon Pask, Stafford Beer, and Humberto Maturana. There appeared to be a tacit understanding that, whatever their differences, they all had a reflexive sense of responsibility for their being in the world and were united in their commitment to a common good.

The concerns with the epistemology of the observer and her responsibilities as a constructor of self-referential, reflexive theories – theories about herself – were made explicit in a coming together of ideas in the late 1960s and early 1970s. I have alluded to some of these events in more detail elsewhere (Scott, 1996, 2004). What I have in mind are Spencer-Brown's (1969)

Laws of Form, which emphasises the primacy of the act of making a distinction; Gordon Pask's articulation of a cybernetic theory of conversations (Pask, 1975b); Gunther's (1971) concept of life as polycontexturality: the intersection of observers' perspectives, including perspectives of others' perspectives; von Foerster's distinction between a first order cybernetics, the study of observed systems, and a second order cybernetics, the study of observing systems (von Foerster et al, 1974, p. 1); Maturana's (1970) arguments for the closure of the cognitive domain based on an account of the operational closure of the nervous system. (I elaborate on these developments in the parts that follow.)

In 1972, Oliver Wells, editor of the cybernetics newsletter, *Artorga*,[4] convened the world's first conference on self-referential systems, in London. The participants were Gotthard Gunther, Gordon Pask, Humberto Maturana, Dionysius Kallikourdis, and myself. Heinz von Foerster was unable to attend. I was fortunate to meet him, later that year, when he visited Pask's laboratory at System Research Ltd., where, following graduation, I had been invited back to work as a research assistant, and at Brunel University, where I was a postgraduate student in cybernetics.

I understood from Ashby (1956) that the abstract principles, concepts, and laws of cybernetics can be applied to any category of system. From Pask, Stafford Beer, Frank George, and others, I understood the role of models and analogies in cybernetics. I saw the power to be found in formal concepts and therefore studied set theory, formal logic, and the theory of computation. I acquired new distinctions and new terminology: hierarchy and heterarchy; object language and metalanguage; programming and meta-programming; process and product; serial, parallel and concurrent processes; circularity and recursion; self-organisation and autopoiesis; variety and information; structure and organisation ... and more.

As a transdiscipline, cybernetics empowered me to cross disciplinary boundaries. This was exhilarating. I also understood other transdisciplines (systems theory, Alfred Korzybski's general semantics, synergetics) to be quite cognate with cybernetics and, at a high enough level of abstraction, homomorphic if not isomorphic with it.

I was inspired, eventually, to regard myself as being a cybernetician. Louis Couffignal (1960, p. 1) defines cybernetics as "L'art d'assurer l'efficacité de l'action" (the art of assuring the efficacy of action). Heinz von Foerster states

---

4 There is an archive of 32 issues of *Artorga* here: https://wellcomelibrary.org/item/b20219490#?c=0&m=0&s=0&cv=0&z=-0.1422%2C-0.0403%2C1.2843%2C0.8068 (accessed 21/07/2017). Many issues contain preprints of articles by renowned early cyberneticians. Pask was a subscriber, so I had the opportunity to read them.

that "Life cannot be studied *in vitro*, one has to explore it *in vivo*." (von Foester 2003, p. 248) and "At any moment we are free to act towards the future we desire" (von Foerster 2003, p. 206). I took these ideas to heart. There was a coming together of my professional life and my personal life, which had previously been lived in separate compartments. I became reflexively aware that I was living my theories and my lived experiences were helping my theorising.

3 *Growing Up*

My 20s and 30s, as for many in the 1960s and 1970s, were an intense period of intellectual and personal exploration in which I was sustained, sometimes tenuously, by the faith in God that I had acquired as a child and my deepening understanding and appreciation of cybernetics. I read widely, acquainting myself with Western philosophy, world history, including the history of science and mathematics, and, in a somewhat haphazard way with the teachings of various faiths ('great' and esoteric) and writings about the 'occult' and shamanism.

In those years, second-order cybernetics was a touchstone that provided rational grounding. With its help, together with the insights of Ludwig Wittgenstein (1953), in particular his meta-philosophic comments about language and philosophy, I escaped from becoming enmeshed in the conceptual and terminological morass of what is frequently referred to as 'continental philosophy'. Cybernetics helped me see through the tricks and power plays of intellectual 'gamesters'.[5] Second-order cybernetics tells us that anything said is said by or to an observer (Maturana, 1970, p. 4; von Foerster, 2003, p. 283). This gives a pragmatic immediacy to what is being said and what is the intention of the communicator. I became a cybernetic shaman, a 'warrior of the spirit', a child of the living God, who aspires to know the true and the good and to be impeccable. I was particularly inspired by the writings of Lao Tsu and Confucius and their followers. At heart, I remained a Christian. In 1979, while training to be a schoolteacher, I summed up much of my thinking and practice in a brief essay, "Morality and the cybernetics of moral development" (Scott, 1983). It has taken a lifetime to appreciate that, however well one understands ancient teachings, one has to learn how to practice them.

Not everyone who studies cybernetics becomes a cybernetician who studies 'the cybernetics of cybernetics'. There are many scholars of cybernetics who look on only from their main area of practice and position themselves in the first instance as being historians, philosophers, architects, biologists,

5 For a masterly critique of the intellectual failings of several of these modern day 'philosophes', see Scruton (2015).

sociologists, psychologists, and so on. In doing so, I believe they miss the point, the sense of what it is to be a cybernetician and a member of the cybernetics community. A recent example is the philosopher and historian Andrew Pickering's (2010) book, *The Cybernetic Brain*, which is in many ways an excellent text. However, Pickering gives a perfunctory, somewhat derogatory treatment of second order cybernetics in general and of Pask's conversation theory in particular. I have similar reservations about the recent (2016) biography of Warren McCulloch by Tara Abraham, *Rebel Genius*, in which the author seems to see McCulloch's enthusiasm for cybernetics as a transdiscipline to be self-aggrandising and self-deceiving.[6] I, myself, share McCulloch's enthusiasm. The invention and creation of a new transdiscipline concerned with control and communication, cybernetics, was itself a great cybernetic achievement.

4 *Concluding Comments*

As an undergraduate, encountering cybernetics transformed my approach to studying and understanding psychology. It gave psychology a conceptual coherence that, previously, I had found lacking.[7] In later years, as my understanding of cybernetics deepened, I continued to use cybernetics as a foundation and framework for my work as an experimental psychologist (summarised in Scott, 1993) and my later work as a practitioner in educational psychology (Scott, 1987) and in educational technology (Scott, 2001). As already noted, the transdisciplinary and metadisciplinary nature of cybernetics empowered me to read widely in other disciplines.[8] I learned from von Foerster that

> Social cybernetics must be a second order cybernetics – a *cybernetics of cybernetics* – in order that the observer who enters the system shall be allowed to stipulate his own purpose [...] [If] we fail to do so, we shall provide the excuses for those who want to transfer the responsibility for their own actions to somebody else.
>
> VON FOERSTER, 2003, p. 286

6 Oddly, Abraham's account of McCulloch's life includes little of his activities as a cybernetician amongst fellow cyberneticians. There is no mention of his significant encounters with Heinz von Foerster, Stafford Beer and Gordon Pask, and his achievements in obtaining funding for cybernetics related research. See McCulloch (1965).

7 In Scott (2016), I sum up my thinking about how cybernetics can provide conceptual foundations for psychology.

8 Apropos of this, the developmental psychologist, Jean Piaget (1977, p. 136), writes, "Thus cybernetics is now the most polyvalent meeting place for physicomathematical sciences, biological sciences, and human sciences."

After some fifty years of involvement with cybernetics, I am more than ever persuaded of its value for making sense of the world and as an aid for self-steering. Ashby's Law of Requisite Variety ("Only variety can destroy variety") makes clear in the simplest terms that if a system is to survive in a changing environment it must manage the variety that it faces. It must learn to identify and minimise unnecessary constraints on its actions. For humans, this applies not only to the first order variety to be found in our environmental niches but also to the second order bewildering 'wicked'[9] complexity of variety to be found in our belief systems and in our perceptions and meta-perceptions of each other. I have written about these issues elsewhere (Scott, 2012). Here, I just wish to emphasise the need for what I refer to as 'education for cybernetic enlightenment.' I have outlined the curriculum for such an education in Scott (2011c).

Discussions about how best to place cybernetics within educational curricula have been going on since shortly after its inception. The (now defunct) Department of Cybernetics at Brunel University where I studied for my PhD had postgraduate students only, arguing that one needed to have a strong disciplinary base before embarking on transdisciplinary studies. In contrast, I am a supporter of Jerome Bruner's concept of the 'spiral curriculum': "A curriculum as it develops should revisit the basic ideas repeatedly, building upon them until the student has grasped the full formal apparatus that goes with them" (Bruner, 1960, p. 13); "We begin with the hypothesis that any subject can be taught effectively in some intellectually honest form to any child at any stage of development." (ibid, p. 33). It makes sense to me – and I hope to the reader – that cybernetic understandings of educational processes should be used to help educate for cybernetic enlightenment. I also believe that cybernetic understandings of the human condition reveal how vital it is that those same understandings are promulgated, not just in formal educational settings, but universally, as part of the 'global conversation'.

Part 3 The Story of Cybernetics

1 *Introduction – Beginnings*

I am not aware of any single text that gives a clear and comprehensive account of the origins, early years, and later key events concerning cybernetics. Here, I will

9 I refer here to 'wicked problems', defined as those that are difficult or impossible to solve because of incomplete, contradictory, and changing requirements that are often difficult to recognize. The use of the term 'wicked' here has come to denote resistance to resolution, rather than evil. See https://en.wikipedia.org/wiki/Wicked_problem (accessed 19/07/2017).

give a very brief summary. As further reading, I suggest Heims (1991), Glanville (2002), Pickering (2010), Scott (2002a, 2004), and Mueller A. and Mueller K. H. (eds.) (2007). I also recommend the (2006) biography of Norbert Wiener, written by Flo Conway and Jim Siegelman. One should also consult key texts of the founders and early contributors: Wiener (1948), Ashby (1956), Pask (1961), von Foerster, Mead et al (1953), Bateson (1972b), Beer (1967).

The story of cybernetics has several possible beginnings. One common starting point is the publication, in 1943, of the paper 'Behavior, purpose and teleology' by Arturo Rosenblueth, Norbert Wiener and Julian Bigelow, and the associated discussions which led up to the Macy conferences on 'feedback and circular causality in biological and social systems' held between 1946 and 1953. The paper proposed that the goal-seeking behaviour that could be built into mechanical systems and the goal-seeking observed in biological and psychological systems have a similar form: they are structured so that signals about achieved outcomes are 'fed back' to modify inputs so that, in due course, a prescribed goal is achieved (a cup is picked up) or a desired state of affairs (the temperature of a room or a living body) is maintained. This process is referred to as 'circular causality'. It was recognised at an early stage that many fields of study contain examples of these processes and that there was value in coming together in multidisciplinary fora to shed light on them, to learn from each other, and to develop shared ways of talking about these phenomena, so the Macy conferences were convened. In 1948, Norbert Wiener, one of the participants, wrote a book that set out these ideas in a formal, coherent way that collected together many of the emerging shared conceptions. The ideas not only facilitated interdisciplinary exchanges but also stood as a discipline in their own right: an abstract transdiscipline: the study of 'control and communication in the animal and the machine'. Wiener called this new discipline, 'cybernetics'. Following the book's publication, the Macy conference participants referred to their conferences as conferences on cybernetics, keeping 'feedback and circular causality in biological and social systems' as a subtitle.

The participants looked for the general forms to be found in the dynamics and organisation of complex systems (living systems, small groups and communities, cultures and societies): how they emerge and develop, how they maintain themselves as stable wholes, how they evolve and adapt in changing circumstances. The term 'self-organising system' was adopted by many as a central topic for discussion in later conferences (for example, Yovits and Cameron, eds., 1960).

In the years following the Macy conferences, cybernetics flourished and its ideas were taken up in many disciplines. Cyberneticians also found common ground with the followers of Ludwig von Bertalanffy, who were developing a general theory of systems (Bertalanffy, 1950, 1972).

2 Later Years – Decline and Renewal

By the 1970s, cybernetics had become marginalised. Several reasons have been suggested for this. I believe two are particularly pertinent. The first is that, at heart, most scientists are specialists. Having taken from cybernetics what they found valuable, they concentrated on their own interests. Second, in the USA, funding for research in cybernetics became channelled towards research with more obvious relevance for military applications, notably research in artificial intelligence.[10]

The early cyberneticians were sophisticated in their understanding of the role of the observer. In the later terminology of Heinz von Foerster, their concerns were both first order (with observed systems) and second order (with observing systems). It is the observer who distinguishes a system, who selects the variables of interest and decides how to measure them. For complex, self-organising systems, this poses some particular challenges. Gordon Pask, in a classic paper, "The natural history of networks" (Pask, 1960), spells this out particularly clearly. Even though the behaviour of such a system is considered to be determined by its current state and the perturbations that affect it, its behaviour is unpredictable: the observer is required to continually update her 'reference frame', that is, to add new possibilities and dimensions. To do so, she must become a participant observer. (As an example, consider the challenges entailed in predicting the behaviour of a cat.) Pask cites the role of a natural historian as an exemplar of what it means to be a participant observer. A natural historian interacts with the system she observes, looking for regularities in those interactions. Pask goes as far as likening the observer's interaction with the system with that of having a conversation with the system. Below, we will see how this insight of Pask became a seed for the development of his cybernetic theory of conversations.

The early cyberneticians also had the reflexive awareness that, in studying self-organising systems, they were studying themselves, as individuals and as a community. Heinz von Foerster, in a classic paper from 1960, "On self-organising systems and their environments", (reprinted in von Foerster, 2003), makes this point almost as an aside. He notes: "When we consider ourselves to be self-organising systems, we have to accept that introspection does not permit us to decide whether the world as we see it is 'real' or just a phantasmagory, a dream, an illusion of our fancy," (von Foerster, 2003, pp. 3–4). Here, von

10 For more on this story, see Umpleby (2003).

Foerster is acknowledging that a self-organising system does not have direct access to an external reality, rather, the 'reality' it computes (constructs) is a consequence of its interactions with its environment. Von Foerster escapes from solipsism by asserting that an observer who distinguishes other selves must concede that, as selves, they are capable of distinguishing her. 'Reality' exists as the shared reference frame of two or more observers. In later papers, with elegant, succinct formalisms, von Foerster, shows how, through its circular causal interactions with its environmental niche and the regularities (invariances) that it encounters, an organism comes to construct its reality as a set of 'objects' and 'events',[11] with itself as its own 'ultimate object'. He goes on to show how two such organisms may construe each other as fellow 'ultimate objects' and engage in communication as members of a community of observers.

As noted in part 2, this interest in the role of the observer and the observer herself as a system to be observed and understood lead von Foerster to propose a distinction between a first and second order cybernetics, where first order cybernetics is 'the study of observed systems' and second order cybernetics is 'the study of observing systems' (von Foerster et al, 1974, p. 1). Von Foerster also referred to this second order domain as the 'cybernetics of cybernetics'.[12] Others had been thinking along somewhat similar lines to those of Pask and von Foerster. Humberto Maturana in his seminal paper, 'Neurophysiology of cognition' (Maturana, 1970), frames his thesis about the operational closure of the nervous system[13] with an epistemological metacommentary about what this implies for the observer, who, as a biological system inhabiting a social milieu, has just such a nervous system. The closure of the nervous system makes clear that 'reality' for the observer is a construction consequent upon her interactions with her environmental niche (Maturana uses the term 'structural coupling' for these interactions). In other words, there is no direct access to an 'external reality'. Each observer lives in her own constructed universe.

---

11 Von Foerster refers to these constructions as 'eigenbehaviours'. See also part 4.

12 Many theorists invoke a third (or higher) order cybernetics and do so in a variety of ways. Of this possibility, although it may be done, von Foerster states, "It would not create anything new, because by ascending into 'second-order', as Aristotle would say, one has stepped into the circle that closes upon itself. One has stepped into the domain of concepts that apply to themselves" (von Foerster, 2003, p. 301).

13 The nervous system is an example of a circular causal system: it is a sensorimotor system in which what is done (motor 'outputs') affects what is sensed (sensory 'inputs') and what is sensed affects what is done (Dewey, 1986). It is also worth noting (as stressed by von Foerster) that all sensing is a form of acting (sensory nerve cells are primed to send signals to other nerve cells when something happens that may be relevant for the whole system of which they are a part) and all acting includes sensing (by proprioception and kinaesthesia) of what is being done. See figure 14 in part 8.

It is by consensus and coordinated behaviour that a shared world is brought forth. As Maturana succinctly points out, 'Everything that is said is said by an observer to an observer who could be him/herself' (Maturana and Varela, 1980, p. 1). In later writings, Maturana uses the term 'autopoiesis' (Greek *autopoiesis*, self-production) to refer to what he sees as the defining feature of living systems: the moment by moment reproduction of themselves as systems that, whatever else they do (adapt, learn, evolve), must reproduce themselves as systems that reproduce themselves. In explicating his theory of autopoiesis, Maturana makes an important distinction: the distinction between the 'structure' of a system and the 'organisation' of a system. A system's structure is the configuration of its parts at a given moment in time: a snapshot of the system's state. The organisation of a system is the set of processes that are reproduced by circular causality such that the system continues to exist as an autonomous unity.[14] In general, a system with this 'circular causal' property is said to be 'organisationally closed'.[15]

In later years, von Foerster refined the concept of a self-organising system, citing the concept of autopoiesis as a useful way to speak about an organism as an autonomous entity: "Autopoiesis is that organization which computes its own organization"; "Autopoietic systems are thermodynamically open but organizationally closed" (Von Foerster, 2003, p. 281). I believe von Foerster's definitions are a very useful way of uniting the earlier and later literatures.
With second order cybernetics, the observer explains herself to herself in a (potentially) never-ending spiral of narratives and conversations – agreements, disagreements, understandings, and misunderstandings - in search of justifiable evidence and logical coherence. In figure 1, the observer (represented by the eye), goes around the circle first time as a naïve realist. At the 9 o'clock point, the observer realises that she, in studying the world around her, has been studying herself. She, too, is an energetically open system (she eats her breakfast) and she, too, is an organisationally closed system. All her knowledge of the world around her, and of herself, is a construction. The perturbations she has experienced have helped her to become 'in-formed' of her world. She now has 'forms' within, which give her world meaning. As von Foerster (2003, p. 189) puts it, "The environment contains no information. The environment is as it is." Sadly, many scientists talk of 'meaning-carrying'

14 Varela, Maturana et al (1974) present a computer program model of autopoiesis.

15 Varela (1979, p. 55) makes the generalisation from the 'autopoiesis' of living systems to the 'organisational closure' of any system that is deemed to be autonomous.

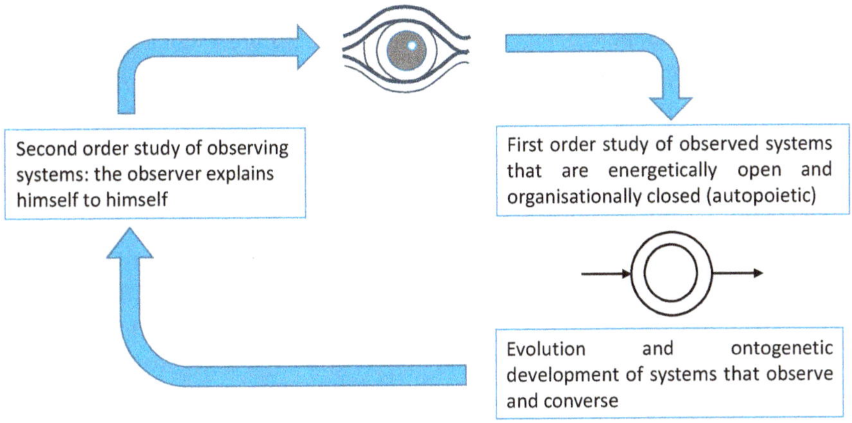

FIGURE 1 Epistemology of the observer: circularity in the domain of explanation

or 'information-carrying' events.[16] They do not realise that these are 'after the event' attributions made by the observer.

Explanation of self and the world is never complete. As Pask (1969a) points out, although life is ineffable and ineluctable, these limits should not be taken as a reason for despair, rather they show the open-ended and creative nature of our attempts to understand ourselves and the world we live in. We can hope for deeper and better understandings of what it is to be human.

Pask, Maturana, Gunther, von Foerster, and other cyberneticians met regularly, often at von Foerster's Biological Computer Laboratory at the University of Illinois, Pask's System Research Ltd., and academic conferences. I witnessed how, over time, cybernetics was marginalised. I saw the courage and nobility with which the cyberneticians maintained their views and convictions in the face of the criticisms that they were old fashioned, misguided and defunct in the brave new world of artificial intelligence research and the emerging field of 'cognitive science.' In the sister transdiscipline, general systems theory (now referred to as 'systems science'), cybernetics was often seen as a mere specialist subdiscipline concerned with control theory. From the 1970s onwards, the 'new' sciences of complexity studies, system dynamics, and artificial life arose,

16 Von Uexküll (2010) refers to external perturbations as 'meaning-carrying' events. Semioticians refer to them as 'signs'. Pert (1999) refers to the molecules that circulate in the body as 'information-carrying', even though a particular molecule will have different effects depending upon where it arrives in the body.

attracting a new generation of scholars, largely ignorant of the intellectual roots that those sciences have in cybernetics. In cognitive science (psychology, philosophy of mind, robotics), there was an increasing interest in the biology of cognition and 'enactivism' (aka 'enaction'), again, with little awareness of the sources of those ideas.

The lights in this darkness have been several. Notably, there has been an ongoing interest in second order cybernetics, as seen in the journals *Cybernetics and Human Knowing* and *Kybernetes.* I do not have space to do more than mention some of the key players whom I see as the second generation of cyberneticians (I became good friends with many): Stuart Umpleby, Ranulph Glanville, Paul Pangaro, Søren Brier, Albert Mueller, Karl Mueller, Phillip Guddemi, Randall Whitaker. I should also like to draw attention to the achievements of the learned societies that have worked to keep cybernetics alive and well: the UK Cybernetics Society, the American Society for Cybernetics, and Research Committee 51 (on Sociocybernetics) of the International Sociological Association. Of particular note is the influence that second order cybernetics has had on family therapy and individual psychotherapy. There is now a large literature on these topics. A summary is well beyond the scope of this publication. The book by Watzlawick, Beavin et al (1967). is a useful starting point.

3 *Cybernetic Explanation*

A key feature in cybernetic explanations is the use of models.[17] The British cybernetician, Frank George, proposes that a theory is a model together with its interpretation, where a model can be anything: marks on paper, a computer program, a mathematical equation, a concrete artefact (George, 1961, pp. 52-56). The model is a non-linguistic part of the theory.[18] It is a form, a structure, a mechanism that can be manipulated by observers and which maps onto the 'real' system that the theory is concerned with. This is to be contrasted with many so-called 'theories' that are to be found in the social sciences and humanities, where metaphors and analogies are liberally deployed, without formal (non-linguistic) justification. Models are to be found throughout the

17 The British psychologist, Kenneth Craik, regarded as a precursor of cybernetics, wrote a small book, *The Nature of Explanation* (Craik, 1943), in which he proposes that the brain acts to model its environment. Sadly, Craik died in 1945, following an accident.

18 In the philosophy of science, having a non-linguistic component in a theory is known as the 'semantic view' and is distinguished from the 'received view' of logical positivism, in which a theory consists of propositions placed in correspondence with observed facts (Suppe, 1977).

sciences. What makes a model 'cybernetic' is the inclusion of circular causality, for example, in a model of a control system, such as a thermostat.[19]

The mapping between a model and the system modelled has the form of an analogy relation, such as, 'A is to B as C is to D', where A and B are parts or states of the model and C and D are parts or states of the system modelled. There may of course be several such relations. It is also relevant to note that metaphors are abbreviated analogy relations. For example, the term 'The ship of state' is asserting that steering a ship is analogous to governing a nation state. Gordon Pask tersely defines cybernetics as 'The art and science of manipulating defensible metaphors' (Pask, 1975a, p. 3). Not only does this definition capture the idea of constructing and validating models, 'manipulating' carries with it the idea that the observer is in a circular causal relation with the model and the system modelled and the use of the word 'defensible' carries with it the idea that the observer is a member of a community of observers. For more on the use of analogies in cybernetics, see Pask (1963).[20]

4 *Gordon Pask's Conversation Theory*

Here, I give a brief overview of Pask's conversation theory. I refer to it in more detail as it relates to different contexts in later parts. Not only was Pask an early enthusiast of, and contributor to, cybernetics, he also had psychology as the main discipline in which he applied cybernetics. As noted above, at an early stage in his thinking, Pask saw the interactions between an observer and a self-organising system as having the form of a conversation, with both system and observer adapting to and learning about each other.

Although much of what Foerster and Maturana have to say is pertinent to humans, arguably it is Pask, the psychologist, who has given us the most comprehensive cybernetic theory of human cognition and communication. He understands that humans develop and evolve in a social context and that 'consciousness' (L. *con – scio*, with – know) is about both knowing with oneself and knowing with others.[21] Throughout his writings, there is an acknowledgment by Pask of his indebtedness to the Russian psychologist Lev Vygotsky, who argued that, as a child develops, what begins as external speech eventually becomes internalised as inner speech (Vygotsky, 1962).

Central in Pask's research activity was the design of teaching machines and learning environments that interact with a learner, in a conversational manner,

19 For more on cybernetic explanations and cybernetic modelling, see Klir and Valach (1967) and Scott (2000).

20 For more on the use of analogies in science, see Hesse (1966).

21 For more about cybernetic understandings of consciousness, see part 8.

and adapt to the learner's progress to facilitate her learning. As a friend and colleague, Pask was familiar with the work of von Foerster and Maturana, and drew on their ideas in creating conversation theory.[22] Pask's theory is a much more fleshed out and elaborated cybernetic account of human cognition, learning and communication than is to be found in the writings of either von Foerster or Maturana.

I shall begin my account of Pask's theory by disambiguating the terms 'observer' and 'observing system' as used in cybernetic writings. Usually, it is clear from the context that 'observer' refers to a human observer capable of being a member of a community of observers. The term 'observing system' is used more generally to refer to autopoietic systems. A single-celled organism, such as an amoeba, can serve as an example. An amoeba to maintain itself as a unity distinguishes itself from its environment. In its interactions with its environment, it adapts. The form of its organisation changes as a consequence of its interactions (its moment by moment structural coupling). As long as these changes do not affect the organisational closure of the system, the system persists. The amoeba becomes 'in-formed' of its environment. It has a perspective on what is its environment, its 'environmental niche'. There is thus a sense in which to be alive is to be affected and to cognise. Multicellular organisms with nervous systems that afford rapid transmission and receipt of signals and rapid self-referential operations have more complex affective responses and greater cognitive powers.

At an early stage in his theorising, Pask made an analytic distinction between a cognitive system and the 'fabric' or 'medium' which embodies it. This distinction is analogous to the distinction between programs and the computer in which they run. However, unlike the cognitive science and artificial intelligence communities, where the analogy is the basis for the thesis that both brains and computers are 'physical symbol systems', Pask stresses how important it is to take account of the differences between brain/body systems and computing machinery. Computers and programs (their software) do not interact. That is how they are designed. The computer's structure changes as it executes a program's commands but, on termination of the program, the computer returns to its starting state. In contrast, brain/body systems are dynamic, autopoietic systems, whose structure is constantly changing. In Pask's terms, in living systems, there is an interaction between the cognitive system (the

22 When first developed, conversation theory was mainly applied to learning and teaching scenarios. The relevance for other scenarios was implicit. In his later writings, Pask explicitly generalised conversation theory. to all social scenarios. He referred to these new developments as 'interaction of actors (IA) theory' (see, for example, Pask, 1996). For the sake of brevity and simplicity, I have retained 'conversation theory' as a label for all this work.

programs being executed) and its embodiment. A change in the structure of the brain/body system affects cognition. Changes in cognition affect the structure of the brain/body system.

In the early 1970s, Pask adopted a new terminology: he referred to brain/body systems with their 'extensions' (for example, a pencil, a walking stick, a bicycle) as 'mechanical individuals' (M-Individuals). Cognitive systems are referred to as 'psychological individuals' (P-Individuals). M-Individuals are the 'processors' that 'execute' the P-Individuals as cognitive processes. At this point, he made a profound theoretical innovation. He declared that P-Individuals, like M-Individuals, are organisationally closed, self-reproducing systems. They have the form of a named class of programs that write themselves. With this construction, Pask provides a model for self-reference and reflexivity in the cognitive domain.[23,24] It is important to recall that Pask's distinction between P-Individuals and M-Individuals is analytic. It is not a cartesian ontological distinction between mind and matter. It is a distinction that provides a useful way of talking about thought distinct from, but interacting with, its embodiment.

In his studies of human learning and cognition, which lead to the development of his conversation theory (CT), Pask took von Foerster's concept of a self-organising system and made it a cornerstone of his theorising about the dynamics of learning, arguing that humans have a 'need to learn' (Pask, 1968). He refers to his interest in the dynamics of human cognition as 'macrotheory'.[25] In contrast, he refers to his (and colleagues) accounts of how human subjects construct particular cognitive processes as 'microtheory'. Pask (1975b) refers to the processes that constitute a cognitive system as 'concepts'.[26] In mainstream cognitive science, concepts are typically thought of as static representations (frames, templates, scripts) of a class (or category) of entities, for example, the class of all horses. For Pask, concepts are dynamic processes that give rise

23 The most complete accounts of the work of Pask and his colleagues from this period are to be found in Pask (1975b, 1976).

24 In order to avoid some of the confusions a partial or shallow reading of Pask can lead to, I have taken, on occasion, to referring to P-Individuals as 'psychosocial unities' and to M-Individuals as 'biomechanical unities'. Pask himself on occasion referred to CT as a theory of the 'psychosocial' and referred to an embodied P-Individual as a 'social actor' (see, for example, Pask, 1996).

25 Macrotheory is crucially concerned with giving some account of 'awareness' and 'consciousness' as being concerned with seeking variety and the consequent reduction of uncertainty. See part 8.

26 In psychology, some theorists reserve the term 'concept' for humans and the term 'habit' for regularities in animal behaviour; others use 'concept', for all organisms. In his early writings, Pask used the term in the latter sense. In conversation theory, the emphasis is on the human ability to provide verbal explanations of concepts and to exemplify them in performance.

to products.[27] Pask defines a concept 'as a procedure that recalls, recognises, constructs or maintains a relation'. The 'relation' is the product, for example: a name or description recalled, an object recognised, a solution constructed, a state of affairs maintained, in general, a goal achieved. He goes on to note that, recursively, there are concepts whose products are other concepts.[28] This affords the construction of hierarchies of concepts. When solving a problem or acquiring a skill, such as riding a bicycle, there are higher level concepts that, guided by feedback about success or failure, construct and select amongst lower level concepts. In this sense, learning is an evolutionary process.[29]

The micro and macro aspects of Pask's theorising are married in the idea that 'conceptualisation', Pask's term for the process of creating and recreating concepts, is an ongoing dynamic activity. A Paskian P-Individual is a system of concepts that is self-reproducing (see figure 2).[30] Particular hierarchies of concepts are temporary constructions and re-constructions within an overall heterarchical, organisationally closed system of processes.[31] Conceptualisation is conserved (one cannot not conceptualise). This is the ongoing process of thinking, imagining and problem solving. Concepts may be refined as new distinctions are made (for example, dogs are distinguished as different breeds). Concepts may be generalised as distinctions are voided (for example, dogs are seen as members of the class, animals). Concepts are applied in particular contexts of action and interaction (as examples: cycling, doing algebra, playing chess). Pask refers to these different contexts as 'conversational domains'. The domains may be related by analogies that map similarities and differences (for example, chess has similarities with draughts and other games). Awareness of these analogy relations can greatly help learning.

---

27 For a very elegant account of the corresponding dynamics of brain activity, see Freeman (2000).

28 In a similar vein, John Lilly (1974) presents a theory of 'programming and metaprogramming in the human biocomputer'. However, Lilly, unlike Pask, does not employ the concept of 'organisational closure'.

29 For more about conversation theory as a theory of learning, see part 8.

30 It may be helpful to also look at figure 12 in part 6.

31 Within mainstream cognitive science, there have been attempts to develop theories of concept system dynamics. (See, for example, Barsalou, 2012.) Arguably, these accounts are unsatisfactory because they lack the concept of an organisationally closed system. In his account of humans as the 'symbolic species', Terence Deacon (1998) posits that the 'mind' or 'self' has the form of a unity but, unlike Pask, does not provide a model for how such a unity functions. There is, of course, a long history of attempts by psychologists and philosophers to describe 'thinking' using metaphors such as 'the association of ideas' (Aristotle), 'mental chemistry' (J. S. Mill), 'the stream of consciousness' (William James), 'all thinking is in signs' (C. S. Peirce).

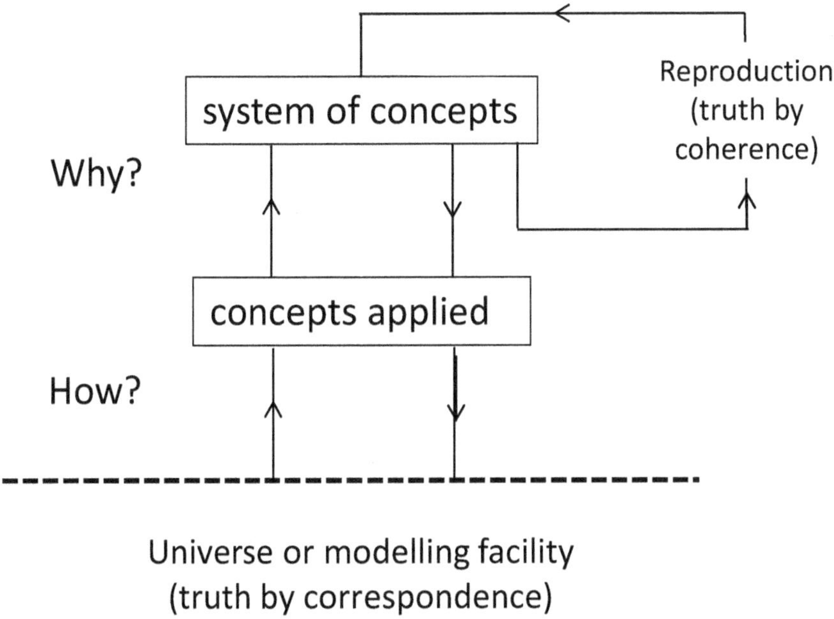

FIGURE 2 A Psychological (P-)Individual is a self-reproducing (coherent) system of concepts

We construct concepts of ourselves and others (see figure 3). We reflect on those concepts: "I am the observed relation between myself and observing myself" (von Foerster, 2003, p. 257). In conversations, the participants conceptualise each other and their perspectives of each other in a 'dance' of reciprocity.[32] Participants 'provoke' (Pask's term) each other to answer questions, explain matters and demonstrate procedures. They teach their understandings back to each other. They agree and may agree to disagree.

In figure 3, the man with the bowler hat is forming concepts of the bald-headed man and the man with the top hat. In doing so, he is contemplating how the man with the top hat perceives others, including how he perceives the man with the bowler hat.

Pask agrees with George Herbert Mead, Leo Vygotsky, Martin Buber and Heinz von Foerster and others that the psychological individual is dialogical in form, *is* a social process, *is* constituted by an inner dialogue, *is* an inner conversation. However, he goes further and asserts that *all conversations have the form of a psychosocial unity, a P-Individual.* This is because the participants are,

32 For more on the dynamics of interpersonal perception, see Scott (1997, 2006). See also the classic work by Laing, Phillipson et al. (1966) and the entry on 'interaction' in part 4.

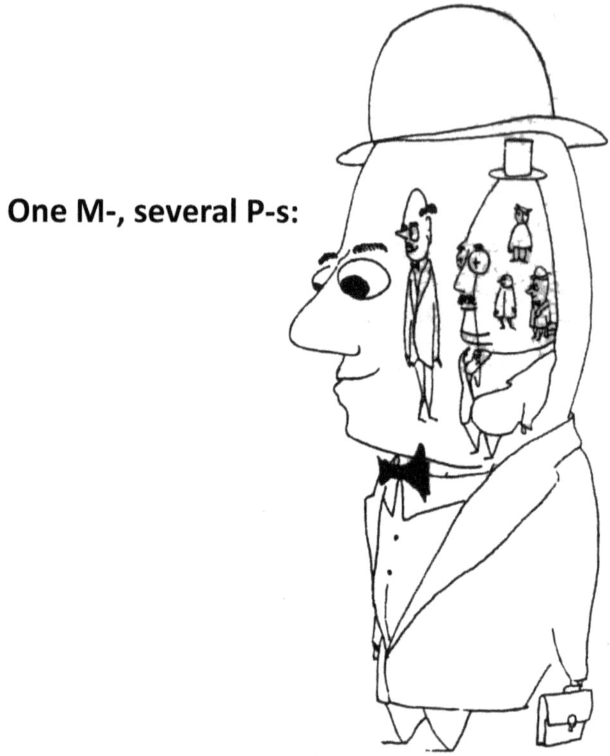

FIGURE 3 Conceptualising self and others (original drawing by Gordon Pask)

for a while at least, conceptualising each other as 'I and thou', and jointly conceptualising themselves as 'we'.

We can now see additional usefulness in making the distinction between M-Individuals and P- Individuals: the two types of unity need not necessarily be in one-to-one correspondence. A single M-Individual may embody several P-Individuals (an inner conversation). A single P-Individual (the outer conversation) may be embodied in several M-Individuals.[33] In the social world at large, embodied psychosocial unities (social actors) take many forms: individual persons, families, organisations, social institutions, and other social systems. All, to some extent at least, are capable of self-observation and reflection, and conversational interaction with other embodied P-Individuals.[34]

33 For an extended discussion of these topics, see Scott (2007, 2009a).

34 Pask (1996) refers to an embodied P-Individual as an 'actor'. Social action takes place in contexts. Contexts are perceived differently by different actors, with tacit or explicit agreements about what the scenarios have in common.

Thus, conversation theory provides an alternative cybernetics-based concept of a social system from that developed by Niklas Luhmann (Luhmann, 1995).[35] These topics are discussed further in later parts, in particular, parts 6, 7 and 12.

Epistemologically, conversation theory is itself reflexive. Top down is the acceptance that theories are the consensual constructions of communities of observers engaged in conversation, including conversations about conversations. As such it is cognate with 'discursive' and 'interpretive' approaches in the social sciences and discussions there of reflexivity and the self.[36] Bottom up, its foundations lie in the cybernetics of self-organising systems and their interactions. Conversation theory can be understood as a theory of theory building that explains its own genesis.

Part 4 Some Key Concepts of Cybernetics

As promised in part 1, in this part there is a selection of what I see as the core set of concepts that give cybernetics its shape and coherence. For each of the concepts, there is a definition and some commentary with examples. Initially, since the concepts form a mesh of inter-relationships, I listed the concepts alphabetically. However, I have been prevailed upon by a reviewer to provide some ordering to help the reader assimilate the concepts better.

The observer: *An observer distinguishes systems and, by interacting with them, assigns or distinguishes their goals/purposes. She may construct models that explain the system's behaviour. An observer is capable of communicating her observations and goals/purposes to other observers.*

Commentary: With second order cybernetics, the observer herself, as a system, becomes an object of study. Systems that are capable of acting as observers are organisationally-closed. The observer constructs her reality. This carries with it the ethical requirement of being responsible for that reality (von Foerster, 2003).

First and second order cybernetics: *First order: the cybernetics of observed systems, with which the observer's interactions are circular causal. Second order: the cybernetics of observing systems, with which the observer's interactions are circular causal and are also participatory and conversational.*

35 Pask and Luhmann are compared more systematically in Buchinger and Scott (2010). Buchinger (2012) provides an insightful critique of the influences on Luhmann's thought.

36 As examples, see Gergen (1999), Gergen et al (2009), Giddens (1991), Herman, Kempen et al (1992), Wiley (1994), Harré and Moghaddam (2003).

Commentary: The distinction between first order and second order cybernetics was first made by Heinz von Foerster (Foerster et al, 1974). Von Foerster's distinction makes explicit what was imminent in the thought of the early cyberneticians. They were aware of the role the observer plays in distinguishing systems. It took von Foerster to make explicit the idea that the cybernetic observer is obliged to "enter the domain of her own descriptions" and acknowledge that she, too, is a self-organising, organisationally closed system. As such, there are limits to what she can ever know about the whole of which she is a part. It behoves her to acknowledge that the reality she subscribes to is one she herself has constructed. Consequentially, she should take responsibility for being the constructer.

System: *Systems are attributes of observers; they are what observers observe. When an observer observes a system, she distinguishes it. She places a boundary around it; she makes it distinct. A system is experienced as something which persists (Ashby, 1956). That which is not a system is experience unqualified, unreflected upon, lacking any distinction, the void.*

Commentary: Following Spencer-Brown, the simplest model for a system is a mark on paper that represents or stands for the system as a circle or other closed curve. Note the complementary aspects of the operation of drawing a distinction. On the one hand, there is the process, what the observer does, on the other hand, there is the product, what she produces.

System (stability and change): *A system is stable if it persists in the context of changes that affect it.*

Commentary: Following Ashby (1956) and others, the classical way of defining a system is in terms of a set of variables that the observer selects as relevant. Together, the possible values of variables form a multi-dimensional space (a 'product set') known as the observer's reference frame or the system's state space. There will be a subset of these values (a 'relation') that defines a system's possible states. Variables whose values must remain within certain limits for the system to persist are referred to by Ashby as 'essential variables'. A path through these states is called a trajectory. If the system is stable, the trajectories converge to an 'attractor', a fixed point, or to a 'basin', a subset of states, that the system cycles through. A non-linear system may converge to a 'strange attractor', a spiral-like cycle that never quite repeats itself.

System (wholes and parts): *A system is a set of interacting or interdependent components forming a unitary whole. An observer distinguishes a system as an ensemble of parts such that, in some measurable/definable way, the whole is greater than the sum of its parts. The distinction is made in the context of an observer's goal/purpose. The observer may assign or discover a goal/purpose for the system. A system that is also an observing system may set a goal/purpose for itself. A system has a boundary that separates it from its environmental niche. It* *has internal processes (its parts interact). A system behaves. As it does so, there are changes to its internal state.*

Commentary: For Ashby (1956), the terms 'system' and 'machine' are treated as synonyms. He goes on to say that a machine is that which persists. Ashby also states that cybernetics is primarily interested in systems that are open to energy and closed to information and control, systems that are 'information tight', living systems being the prime examples.

Constraint: *A constraint refers to any limitations on a system's possible states, behaviours or processes.*

Commentary: Constraints may be internal to the system, imposed by limits on the forms it may take whilst maintaining itself as an organisation. Constraints may be external to the system, imposed by the topology and other properties of its environmental niche.

Variety (order, redundancy): *Variety is an observer's measure of the possible states a system may occupy and the behaviours it may exhibit in particular contexts. Order/redundancy refers to the extent to which a system's states and behaviours are predictable. The Law of Requisite Variety states that "Only variety can destroy variety", that is, the variety of states and behaviours available to the controller must exceed those available to the controlled.*

Commentary: The Law of Requisite Variety was first formulated by Ashby (1956). It is sometimes stated in the form, "Only variety can control variety." As an example, a hunter's behaviour must have more variety than the behaviour of the hunted. If not, the hunter may become the hunted.

Self-organisation: *According to the definition proposed by von Foerster (1960), a self-organising system is one whose rate of change of redundancy is always positive. It is always becoming more organised, capable of a greater variety of internal states and behaviours.*

Commentary: For an observer, the hallmark that a system is self-organising is that she has to continually update her reference frame for the system. A self-organising system is organisationally closed. Von Foerster and other cyberneticians have biological and social systems in mind as exemplars of self-organisation. The physicist, Ilya Prigogine, uses the term 'self-organisation' to refer to the 'coherent space-time structures at the macro level' that emerge in far from equilibrium physical and chemical systems as they dissipate energy, for example, eddies and whirlpools in flowing water (Prigogine, 1980). Such structures are not organisationally closed. Rather, they are necessary precursors in the evolution of life.

Organisational closure/Autopoiesis: *An observer distinguishes a system as organisationally closed if the products of the processes of the system include the processes themselves, i.e., the system, as an organisation, is self-productive.*

Maturana and Varela (1980) refer to living systems that are organisationally closed as autopoietic (self-producing) systems.

Commentary: Note that here we have a case of not only the observer distinguishing a system but the system distinguishing itself by computing and maintaining its own boundary. As described on p. 26, Maturana makes a distinction between the 'structure' of a system and the 'organisation' of a system. A system's structure is the configuration of its parts at a given moment in time: a snapshot of the system's state. The organisation of a system is the set of processes that are reproduced by circular causality such that the system continues to exist as an autonomous unity. An organisationally closed system can be modelled as a strange attractor: always changing its structure but always maintaining its organisation.

Linear/nonlinear systems; trivial/nontrivial systems; complicated/complex systems

The above terms are related and are used in a variety of ways in cybernetics and beyond. Here, I do my best to explain them, whilst avoiding formal, technical language.

A linear system is in principle predictable. This is because the output is proportional to the input: changes in input bring about corresponding changes in output. It is also the case that if different inputs are added together so are the corresponding outputs. One may say, "The whole is the sum of the parts." A nonlinear system is one that is not linear. It is one where' "The whole is more than the sum of the parts."

Commentary: Except in some special cases, nonlinear systems are not predictable. The usual technique for achieving predictability is to use a linear model to approximate the behaviour of the nonlinear system. Examples of nonlinear systems include the weather, the stock market, and, by definition, any system that is self-organising.

A trivial system is one that has been constructed to be – or rendered to be – predictable. A non-trivial system is not predictable.

Commentary: The terms 'trivial system' and 'nontrivial system' were first used in cybernetics by Heinz von Foerster. In an early paper (von Foerster, 2003, pp. 133–167), he mocks experiments on animals in behavioural psychology as ones in which, using a training routine, an unpredictable self-organising system (a rat or a pigeon) is rendered predictable, i.e., a nontrivial system is made to behave as if it were a trivial system. Throughout his career, von Foerster caricatured conventional education regimes as ones in which nontrivial systems are made to become trivial systems: creative, adventurous students are obliged to be conformist and controllable. Von Foerster illustrates his distinction by showing how simple machines can be programmed to be trivial or nontrivial. A trivial machine is one where the internal state is held constant (it plays no determining role), thus the output is solely determined by the input. In behaviourist terms, the 'stimulus' determines the 'response'. A nontrivial machine is one where the output is a function of (determined by) the input and the present internal state, and where the next internal state is also a function of its present internal state and its input.

To relate the terms trivial/nontrivial and linear/nonlinear, we can note that a trivial system is an example of a linear system and a nontrivial system is an example of a nonlinear system.

A complicated system has many inputs, outputs, and internal states or parts. However, it can, in principle, be analysed and its behaviour predicted. A complex system is one that is unpredictable or only partially predictable.

Commentary: The concepts of complexity and complex system, which originated in cybernetics, have taken on a life of their own. In biology, the physical sciences, and computer science, definitions are reasonably clear.[37] However, in the social sciences and the humanities, the terms are often used in metaphorical and mystifying ways which seem to add little to the arguments being made.[38] [39] To keep things simple, I suggest the simple rubric that linear systems may be complicated but only nonlinear systems are complex.

Control: *Control refers to the system's processes that use feedback about error to achieve the system's goals/purposes. At any instant, the interactions of the controller and the controlled are mutually affecting. Thus, the distinction the observer makes between the controller and the controlled is one of her choosing.*

Figure 4 is a (very) simple model of a control process. The controller has an environment on which it acts (or operates) in pursuit of some goal. It receives feedback about the effect of its operation. The feedback helps determine what it should do next. At this high level of abstraction, controllers may also be referred to as regulators, problem solvers, teachers, managers, steerers, designers, and

37 See, for example, John Holland's primers *Emergence: From Chaos to Order* (1998) and *Complexity: A Very Short Introduction* (2014), and James Gleick's (1988) *Chaos: Making a New Science*.

38 Other terms which have left their precise mooring in the technical disciplines include 'chaos' and 'emergence'. See Urry (2003) for one out of many possible examples of this kind of usage.

39 One misuse of a precise term that I find annoying is the liberal use of the expression 'at the edge of chaos'. In physics one might meet the example of a pot of water that is simmering, not yet boiling, as a precise, measurable instance of a system 'at the edge of chaos'. By analogy, one could say that the whole biosphere, in so far as it supports life, is 'at the edge of chaos', i.e., thanks to the sun, it is not too hot and not too cold.

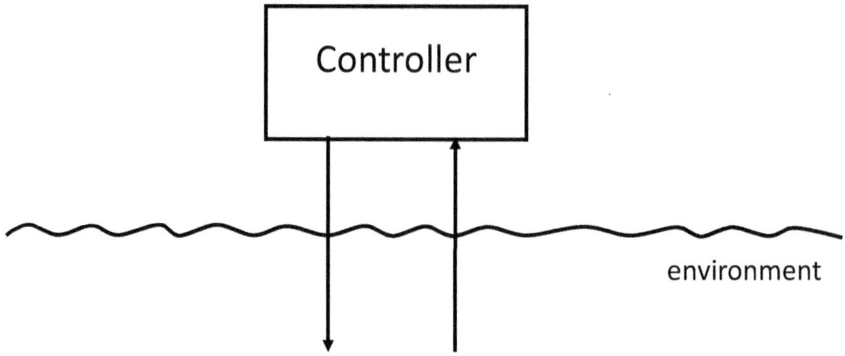

FIGURE 4 A control process

creators. Their operations may be to construct something (bring about a state of affairs), to recognise or recall something, or to maintain a state of affairs.

Control processes may be organised hierarchically, where higher-level controllers control lower-level controllers by setting their goals and other defining parameters, such as how sensitive they are in responding to feedback (see figure 5). Higher-level control may be thought of as the operation of selecting amongst a population of putative lower-level controllers. It may also be thought of as the construction of lower-level controllers. In all cases, the higher-level controllers require feedback about the effectiveness of the lower-level controllers. In this context, Ashby (1956) refers to the use of hierarchies of regulators as a way of 'amplifying intelligence'. Pask (1975a) refers to learning as the construction of a hierarchy of problem solvers. John Holland (1975) models adaptation as a process where there is selection from a population of 'genetic algorithms', that are constructed using the random assortment of components, analogous to the recombination of genes observed in meiosis (part of sexual reproduction). Control may also be distributed *heterarchically*, as a set of interacting controllers.

Hierarchy and heterarchy: *A system may be distinguished and modelled by an observer as being hierarchical, i.e., as having an overall controller with subordinate (sub-)controllers. Alternatively, it may be distinguished and modelled as being heterarchical, i.e., as consisting of interacting parts where there is no fixed overall controller and where, at any instant, the part which can best achieve the system's goals/purposes takes control.*

Commentary: The hierarchical structure of many complex systems (social, biological, artificial) has been highlighted by several authorities. Simon (1962) is a classic paper on this topic. The term 'heterarchy' was coined by McCulloch (1965) to describe how the mammalian nervous system is organised to rapidly

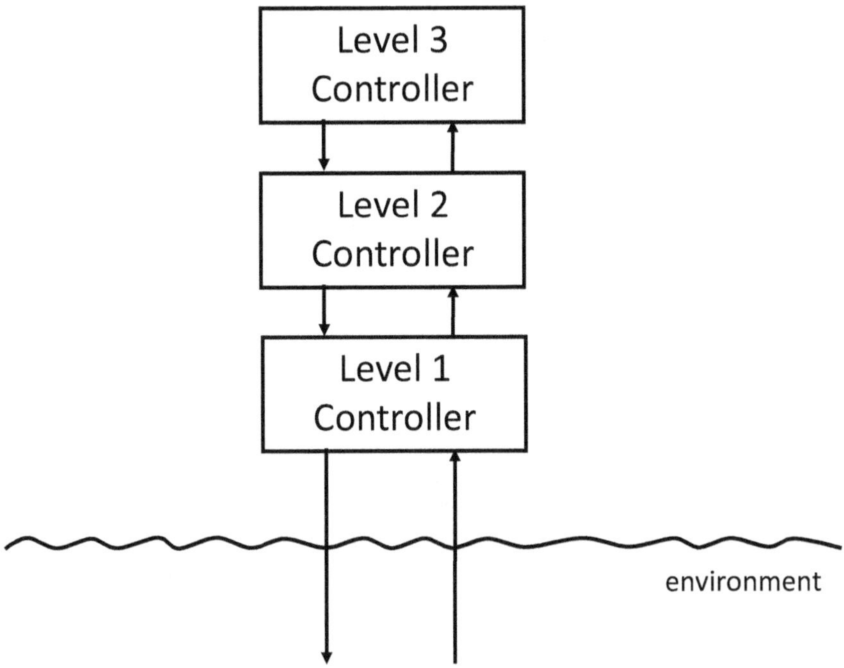

FIGURE 5 A control hierarchy

adopt the most appropriate behavioural mode. Examples of these modes are: fight, flee, eat, sleep, engage in sexual activity, groom. McCulloch and colleagues identified sixteen different modes typically adopted by cats. At any one moment, a particular mode is in command, imposing a particular hierarchical organisation. As circumstances change, a different mode takes over. (See also part 8). McCulloch saw the decision-making processes found in heterarchical systems as a general class of cybernetic processes. He formulated the 'Principle of the Redundancy of Potential Command' which states (my paraphrase): "Command of a system should be taken by the part that has the most relevant information." The word redundancy is used to emphasise that more than one possible commander is available. As another example of this principle, McCulloch cited the command and control system used in the navy before radio was invented, and when communication was by flags and signalling lamps. Although one ship would be occupied by the Admiral of the Fleet, when the ships were sailing in line, it was the ship that had first sight of the enemy that took command.

The two concepts, hierarchy and heterarchy, can be reconciled as follows. A self-organising, autopoietic system is intrinsically heterarchical. Hierarchies of controllers and controlled are temporary structures created and recreated in the pursuit of the goals and subgoals that have been set.

Feedback and circular causality: *A system uses feedback about error to control the achievement of its goals/purposes. Circular causality is a more general notion that refers to (i) internal processes that maintain a system's stability (its persistence) (ii) the interactions of a controller and the controlled.*

Goal/purpose/error: *In attempting to achieve its goal/purposes, a system uses measures of error (deviations from its goals/purposes) as feedback to modify its behaviour to better achieve its goals/purposes.*

Commentary: Here, goal and purpose are viewed as synonyms. Another way of thinking about goals and purposes is that they signify things that have value for the system, things (states of affairs) that the system aims to maintain or achieve. As Glanville (2002) has emphasised, error is a constant feature of life. To be is to be in time and in time things go wrong. He contrasts this with the ideal of an atemporal, eternal world where nothing ever goes wrong. All dynamic systems can be seen as adapting to perturbations to survive and to fulfil their goals. Humans have the additional capability of reflecting on and reasoning about their purposes. They may set goals for themselves. As Pask (1969a) notes, some of these goals may be underspecified, for example, "I'm seeking an adventure." The seeker fills in the details of how to attain the goal as she goes along.

Process and product: *A process refers to system activity whereby its internal state changes and it exhibits behaviours. These changes are referred to as the products of the process.*

Commentary: Pask (1996) has stated a duality principle: "For every process, there is a product; for every product there is a process that produced it." Notice, the product of a process may itself be a process. A mentioned in part 3, Pask refers to cognitive processes as 'concepts'.

Figure 6 is a simple representation of a process, used by Miller, Galanter et al (1960) in their book, *Plans and the Structure of Behaviour*, to model cognitive processes. They refer to it as a TOTE unit, a process with four stages, 'Test, Operate, Test, Exit'. The process begins with a test to see if a given goal has been achieved. If the test is failed, an operation is invoked, followed by a repeat of the test. The cycle of 'Test, Operate, Test' is repeated until the test is passed. When the test is passed, the unit is exited and a further TOTE unit is initiated as part of a chain of processes. An example is hammering a nail into a piece of wood, where the test is to see if the nail is flush with the surface of the wood. Hammering (the operation) is repeated until the test is passed, at which stage the next TOTE unit is initiated. Figure 7 shows how TOTE units may be chained and 'nested'. In the figure, the two lower units are chained together as subgoals of a higher order goal. For example, the second lower unit could have the test, "Is the surface of the wood covered with paint?") and the operation, "Apply

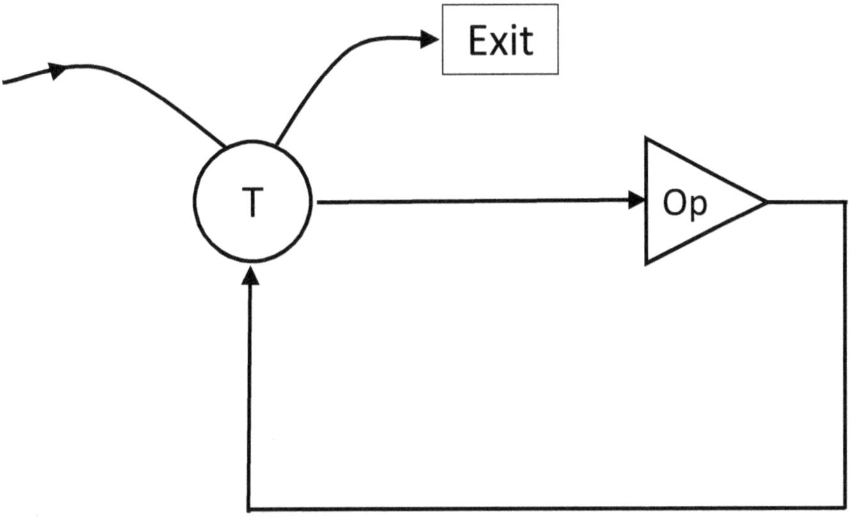

FIGURE 6 A "Test > Operate > Test > Exit" (TOTE) unit

paint". TOTE units can be used to describe complex processes and tasks. For example, a description of how to construct a piece of furniture.

A TOTE unit is isomorphic with the basic form of procedure found in a computer program, an "If, then, else" procedure, where the "If" part is a test, "then" leads to an operation, and "else" leads to the next procedure. You may have already noticed this similarity. Miller, Galanter et al's book (1960) revolutionised cognitive psychology. In their introduction, they describe how they drew inspiration from the new science of cybernetics.

The TOTE unit concept may be generalised in many ways. In the social and behavioural sciences, one has 'norms', 'scripts' and other rule-like structures, which are used to analyse and design the form and behaviour of complex systems, for example, social roles, social institutions, industrial processes.

Note that processes may be executed (occur) serially, that is, one after the other. They may also be executed in parallel, that is, several at the same time but independently of each other. They may also be executed 'concurrently', that is, several at the same time but with the possibility of affecting or interfering with each other as they occur. These distinctions between types of process provide a useful way of distinguishing the natural from the artificial. In artificial systems, for example, a digital computer executing a program, serial processing and parallel processing are the rule. Concurrency is not allowed as it may cause errors. In natural systems, such as brains, bodies and ecosystems, concurrency of processes is ubiquitous. Possible conflicts are resolved in the ongoing dynamics of organisational closure (autopoiesis), where a system is

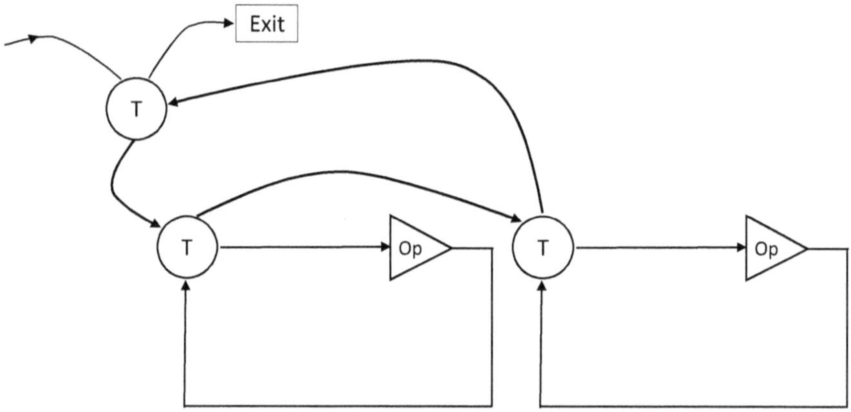

FIGURE 7 Nested TOTE units

the product of the processes that produced it and which continue to maintain it. It is these dynamics that give rise to the emergence of novel forms in adaptation, learning, and evolution. (See also part 8).

Compute/construct/model/map: *Synonyms for the processes by which organisms come to know themselves and their environmental niches as stable realities.*

Commentary: From the inception of cybernetics, cyberneticians have considered how organisms construct their realities as forms of computation, albeit, 'biological computation', involving the 'wetware' of brains and bodies rather than the 'hardware' of man-made computers. It was much later that the term 'constructivism' became current in epistemology and education (Jean Piaget was a major influence on this development). In 1973, Heinz von Foerster, who set up and directed the Biological Computer Laboratory at the University of Illinois, published a seminal paper, "On constructing a reality", which brought the terms, computation and construction, together. The paper is still well worth reading. It has been reprinted as chapter 8 in von Foerster (2003).

Alfred Korzybski develops similar constructivist views in his 'general semantics' He is famous for the aphorism, "The map is not the territory" (Korzybski, 1933 p. 58).

Habit/universal/invariant/object permanence/eigenbehaviour/coordination/concept: *These terms all refer to how organisms construct (compute) a stable reality.*

Commentary: The 19th century philosopher, Charles Saunders Peirce, highlighted the fact that organisms 'take on habits'. This idea became a central theme in behaviourist psychology, where learning is conceived of as the acquisition of habits in the form of connections between stimuli and responses ('stimulus-response bonds'). Warren McCulloch, with his colleague Walter Pitts, wrote a paper, "How we know universals", which showed how a network of simple neuron-like elements could compute 'invariants', things that are considered to be the 'same' whilst being transformed in some way (McCulloch, 1965). For example, an object, such as a bottle, is considered to be the same thing from whatever direction it is perceived. In his studies of child development, Jean Piaget refers to this as 'object permanence'. With his colleague, Barbel Inhelder, he showed that infants are not born with object permanence. They go through a phase of coordinating sensorimotor activities such that object permanence is achieved: they become aware of themselves as objects in a three-dimensional world of objects (Piaget, 1954; Piaget and Inhelder, 1972). Heinz von Foerster, refers to the invariants (regularities, stabilities) that are computed in the recursive (circular) operations of the sensorimotor system[40] as 'eigenbehaviours', a term taken from mathematics ('eigen' is German for 'own', 'proper', 'particular'). In a paper written as a tribute to Jean Piaget (reprinted as chapter 11 in von Foerster, 2003), von Foerster refers to 'objects', as perceived and experienced, as 'tokens for eigenbehaviours' (von Foerster, 2003, p. 261). He goes on to generalise the concept of an eigenbehaviour to include all stabilities that emerge and are observed in individual and collective, consensual, coordinated activity. In similar spirit, Humberto Maturana refers to the recursive coordination of coordinations. Gordon Pask refers to the processes that recognise, recall, construct and maintain 'relations' (stable forms) as 'concepts'. He notes that there are concepts that compute other concepts and that a 'self' is a self-reproducing system of concepts. (See part 3).

Communication: (*i*) *The observer may model interactions between and within observed systems as the transmission and reception of signals* (*ii*) *The observer may model interactions between observing systems as a conversation, where "conversation" refers to the processes whereby two organisationally closed systems* (*the participants*) *interact and construct models* (*concepts, perspectives*) *of each other. This includes the construction of models of each other's models* (*metaperspectives*) *as they learn about each other.*

Commentary: (i) The transmission and reception of signals within and between observed systems is treated in Shannon and Weaver (1949). It is also treated more generally in the first order cybernetics of Ashby (Ashby, 1956). (ii) By modelling each other, systems in conversation can explore their similarities and differences, coordinate their behaviours, and come to know or be 'in-formed' of each other. The coordination may be aided by the use of symbols

40 Sensing is a function of (depends on) motor activity; motor activity is a function of what is sensed.

(uttered, gestured, written) which have (or are intended to have) shared significance. (See below, 'interaction', and part 5.)

Interaction: *Interaction refers to any way in which systems affect each other's states and behaviours. Within a system, interaction refers to how the parts affect each other.*

Commentary: Interaction is a very general term, denoting any occasion when a system's behaviour brings about a reaction that may lead to further interaction. One can usefully distinguish between first order interactions, where systems are observed to be affecting each other, and second order interactions where observers are in conversation and are reflexively aware (conscious) that this is the case.[41] Aspects of the interactions between observers may go unnoticed by one or more of the participants. This depends on how the individual observers are consciously 'reading' the situation, where the situation includes both verbal and non-verbal interaction. In social settings, much interaction happens in habitual ways, without awareness. When one enters a social space, one enters into communication (Birdwhistell, 1970). Watzlawick, Beavin et al. (1967), building on the work of Bateson (1972) and others, propose a set of axioms for the pragmatics of human communication. Strictly, their propositions are not axioms since they are not independent, rather they are maxims. Maxim 1, "One cannot not communicate", captures the insight that the message not sent is also informative. Maxim 2, "One cannot not meta-communicate", notes that messages are always set in a context which is itself a message about the message. Maxim 3, "Messages are either analogical or digital", notes that messages may be encoded in digital or analogue form. Speech and writing use the encoding of natural language, which is doubly digitised in its use of phonemes and morphemes. A picture or bodily gesture expresses messages analogically. Maxim 4, "A message is punctuated differently by sender or receiver", notes that senders and receivers may give different meanings to messages. Maxim 5, "Communication may be symmetrical or complementary", refers to possible power relations between sender and recipient. Symmetrical relationships are peer-peer. Complementary relationships are those of commander-commanded, for example, employer-employee, parent-child.

Inspired by these maxims, I have proposed a set of maxims for power relations, where an 'agenda' is defined as "The set of goals and subgoals that a particular participant is pursuing on the occasion of an interaction". The maxims include: "One cannot not have an agenda", "One cannot not have a meta-agenda" (justifications, strategy, tactics), "Relations between agendas may be

41 In sociology, the shared expectation that conversation is possible is referred to as 'double contingency'. For the history of this concept, see Vanderstraeten (2002).

neutral or give rise to positive or negative synergy", "By the principle of the redundancy of potential command, participants who are related heterarchically may adopt hierarchical relations as temporary arrangements for the pursuit of agreed goals", and, vice versa, "Hierarchical relations may be suspended once goals are achieved" (Scott, 2006).

Laing, Phillipson et al.'s (1966) work was one of the first studies of interpersonal perception that articulated how human communication entails both sender and recipient having perspectives of each other's perspectives, i.e., meta-perspectives. The structure in Figure 8 shows the set of perspectives and meta-perspectives for two participants, A and B. In principle, the topic being discussed or the message being interpreted may be anything that can be pointed to or named. For example, the topic, 'most beautiful motor car'. Each participant has a perspective on the topic, a way of describing or explaining the topic. Each participant also has a perspective of the other's perspective. And finally, to give us the required number of levels to exhibit all forms of stability or conflict, each participant has a perspective of the other's perspective of perspectives. In Laing et al.'s original terminology there may be an agreement or not at the base level; at the second level, there may be understanding or not that there is an agreement or not. And at the third level, there may be realisation or not that there is understanding or not about what is happening at the base level.

Laing et al. point out that, as long as at least one of the participants has a correct understanding of the pattern of perceptions and possible misperceptions, then the relationship may be a stable one. The participant with the correct understanding can adapt to the errors in the other participant's perceptions. That same participant may deceive and manipulate to further selfish ends. In Laing et al.'s model for two persons interacting, there are two meta-perspective levels above the base level. Howard's [1971] theory of metagames shows that, in general, if one is to represent all possible configurations of perspectives of perspectives for n persons, it is necessary to have n factorial (n!) levels above the base level.[42] This is one possible reason for error in human communication. We know from studies in cognitive psychology that there is a limit, equal to approximately seven plus or minus two, on the number of "chunks" of data that a human may hold in mind at any one time [Miller, 1956]. Signals containing more variety than this will tend to be condensed, "chunked". Notice that this also applies to how the human actor perceives her social world. In any particular communicative context, she will chunk the participants into

42 For a study involving three persons, requiring the elicitation of seven perspectives per person, see Scott (2008).

A (B (A (T)))	**Level of Realisation or Not**	B (A (B (T)))
A (B (T))	**Level of Understanding or Not**	B (A (T))
A (T)	**Base Level (Agreement or Not)**	B (T)

FIGURE 8 Perspectives and meta-perspectives
Notes: A and B are participants. T is the topic, proposition or object being contemplated or perceived
SOURCE: LAING ET AL. (1966)

subgroups or coalitions to be able to think about them at the same time. Of course, in many cases, participants may already be grouped. However, not all participants will see the same set of groupings being in operation. Each participant will have his or her perception of what is the communicative context.[43]

Laws of Form: In a remarkable contribution to the foundations of logic and mathematics, George Spencer-Brown (1969), formulated the Laws of Form. He begins with the idea of an observer drawing a distinction. His work very soon caught the attention of cyberneticians, who hailed it as a masterpiece. The Laws are:

Axiom 1. The Law of Calling

The value of a call made again is the value of the call.

That is to say. if a name is called and then is called again, the value indicated by the two calls taken together is the value indicated by one of them.

Axiom 2. The Law of Crossing.

The value of a crossing made again is not the value of the crossing.

That is to say, if it is intended to cross a boundary and then it is intended to cross it again, the value indicated by the two intentions taken together is the value indicated by none of them. That is to say, for any boundary to recross is not to cross (Spencer-Brown, 1969, pp. 1–2).

Commentary: "The laws of form have finally been written! ... G. Spencer Brown cuts smoothly through two millennia of growth of the most prolific and persistent of semantic weeds, presenting us with his superbly written laws of form. This Herculean task which now, in retrospect, is of profound simplicity rests on his discovery of the form of laws. Laws are not descriptions, they are commands, injunctions: 'Do!' Thus, the first constructive proposition in this

43 Using Pask's concept of a P-Individual, a conversation involving n persons can be partitioned into $2^n - 1$ conversations. For example, for three persons ABC, the set of possible conversations is {ABC, AB, AC, BC, A, B, C}. This includes the conversations participants have with themselves. Here $2^n - 1 = 2^3 - 1 = 8 - 1 = 7$.

book (page 3) is the injunction: 'Draw a distinction!' an exhortation to perform the primordial creative act. After this, practically everything else follows smoothly: a rigorous foundation of arithmetic, of algebra, of logic, of a calculus of indications, intentions and desires; a rigorous development of laws of form, may they be of logical relations, of descriptions of the universe by physicists and cosmologist, or of functions of the nervous system which generates descriptions of the universe which it is itself a part," Heinz von Foerster's review of *Laws of Form*, in *The Last Whole Earth Catalogue* (1971, p. 12). Available from https://archive.org/details/B-001-013-719/page/n12/mode/1up (accessed, 06/05/2020.)

The book *Laws of Form* is very special. Not everyone 'gets it', including clever mathematicians. For the non-mathematician, the best way to access it is to read the introduction (and maybe also look at the prefaces of whatever edition you have obtained), then read the first three chapters as best as you can, then read the notes for those chapters. Take your time. A knowledge of binary arithmetic from computing may help you see how simple the calculus is. Don't worry if you don't get it at first. Put it to one side and come back to it later. Eventually, one sees the beauty in it.

With the first law, we have the primitive notion of naming, of allowing one thing to stand for another. We also have the notion of redundancy in a message: to name something twice adds nothing to the meaning (the value) of a message. With the second law, we have the primitive notion of action or movement, going from one side of the distinguishing boundary to the other, and possibly back again. Here, things are done and may be undone. Here, the distinction is interpreted as a command to enter the system. The observer's operations of making a distinction – of distinguishing a system – is reversible; he may undo or 'void' his distinction.

Spencer-Brown expresses the two laws as equations (call + call = call; crossing + crossing = no crossing). Using a simple notation,[44] he then develops a 'calculus of indications', showing how complex forms may, step by step, be evaluated as indicating the binary values 'something' or 'nothing', which, depending on the context, may be interpreted as indicating '1 or 0' (arithmetic), 'true or false' (logic) or other binary values, such as inside/outside, present/absent, empty/full, good/bad. The two laws, with their complementarity, capture a fundamental 'philosophic distinction' expressed in a variety of ways: knowing/doing; epistemology/ontology; cognition/volition; describe/coordinate (see also, part 7).

---

44 For examples of the notation, see von Foerster's review https://archive.org/details/B-001-013-719/page/n12/mode/1up.

The calculus also includes an algebra,[45] where some tokens are place holders (variables) for the presence or absence of a value (a constant). When an observer distinguishes a system, she establishes values. With variables (unknowns), she may construct forms whose overall value is contingent on the value of the variables that are part of the form, thus representing possible, (hypothetical) systems, to be constructed or investigated.

With a simple extension to his notation, Spencer-Brown shows that a potentially infinite recursive nesting of forms within forms may be constructed, using finite marks on paper. Spencer-Brown calls this recursive operation, 're-entry'. For potentially infinite forms, he distinguishes a third, 'imaginary' value, one that represents being true or false, of oscillating between presence and absence, of being on or off. Here we have the beginnings of theories of time and space, theories of dynamical systems, their emergence and development, theories of memory, awareness and consciousness.

Part 5 On Messages

1 *Introduction*

> Society can only be understood through a study of the messages and the communication facilities which belong to it; and that in the future development of the messages and communication facilities, messages between man and machines, between machines and man, and between machine and machine, are destined to play an ever-increasing part.
>
> NORBERT WIENER, 1950

In this part, I discuss the concept of 'message' as applied to these different forms of communication: between man and machine, between machine and machine, and between man and man. (As intended by Wiener, 'man' is used as a general noun that includes all human beings; later in the part, to accord with contemporary usage, I use the term 'human'.) As Ludwig Wittgenstein (1953) reminds us, rather than ask what a word means we should look to see how it is used. The term 'message' can refer to a relatively simple cause and effect interaction. An example is the transmission of a mechanical signal, that when decoded by a receiving system, triggers a standard response. It can also refer to the much more subtle and complex case where recipients construct meanings based on the messages

45 Arabic, *al gebra*, the sorting out of broken parts, as in the rules for adding, subtracting, multiplying and dividing fractions.

they receive. I contend that it is only in this latter case that we can properly refer to the interaction as a 'conversation'. In this part, I present cybernetic models of these two usages, messages as codes and messages as constituents of conversations.[46] I go on to discuss the relevance of the code/conversation distinction for the different cases when senders and recipients are human beings or machines. The coding model is presented in section 2. It is the model developed by Claude Shannon and Warren Weaver (Shannon and Weaver, 1949).

The conversation model is presented in section 3. It is taken from Pask's conversation theory (Pask, 1975b, 1976).[47] This model may not be familiar to many cyberneticians or social scientists, so I present it in some detail. In section 4, I pay particular attention to man-machine interaction, noting there are contexts in which such interactions may be usefully considered to be conversational in form and for which the machine 'participant' may be explicitly designed to be a surrogate for a human conversational partner. In section 5, I relate the abstract discussion to some current developments. In section 6, there are some concluding comments.

2 *Communication as Coding*

The Shannon and Weaver model of communication is shown in figure 9. It is what lies at the heart of their so-called 'information theory', which is concerned with measuring the capacity of channels to transmit messages, when the channels may be subject to 'noise' that degrades the messages, and measures of how much 'information' is contained in particular messages. I have put the word 'information' in quotation marks because I, like many other scholars, find the use of the word to be problematic and liable to create conceptual confusion. Given the measures they use (the number of binary decisions or 'bits' needed to code or decode a message),[48] instead of talking about 'information transmission', I believe it would be more appropriate to talk of 'data transmission'. In the model, a message is a sequence of physical events, distinguished by an external observer, that is considered to represent possible symbolic entities (such as noughts and ones, alphanumeric characters, dots and dashes) taken from a finite set and combined according to set rules. The semantics of messages ('meanings') are not considered. In Gregory Bateson's terms, each event

46 The way in which I make this distinction is influenced by how it is made by Ranulph Glanville (Glanville, 1997).

47 Introductions to Pask's work can be found in Scott (1993, 2001, 2007, 2009a).

48 For example, the decimal number 8 is 1000 in binary notation. It requires 4 bits (4 binary choices of 0 or 1) to express it. Reading from the right, the place values show there are no 1s, no 2s, no 4s and one 8. The binary number 1111 also requires 4 bits. Read from the right, there is one 1, one 2, one 4, and one 8 which makes the value in decimal notation 15.

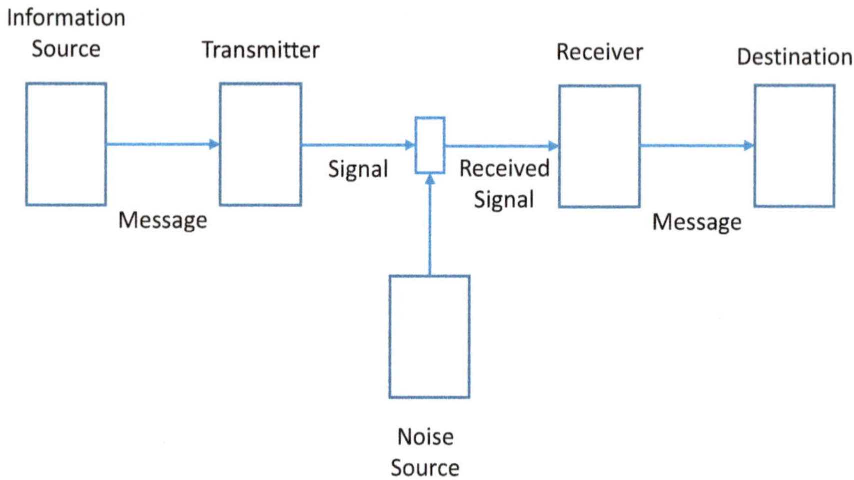

FIGURE 9 The Shannon and Weaver model of communication

is a 'difference' in so far as it is indeed different from other members of the set. Shannon and Weaver's model is thus concerned with how well these differences can be transmitted without degradation.

Critics of this usage of the term 'information' point out that events (the data) should only be considered as informative insofar as their reception brings about relevant (significant, meaningful) changes in the receiving system, i.e., there is some acknowledged pragmatic consequence.[49] As Bateson puts it, "Information is a difference that makes a difference". In a similar spirit, Jerzi Konorski (1962) says, "Information cannot be separated from its utilisation." Examples of differences that make differences are the feedback signals in a control mechanism, such as a thermostat, which indicate whether or not a particular goal has been achieved or maintained. We only know that a signal (a difference) is informative if it does indeed make a difference. (See also footnote 16, page 21.)

3 *Communication as Conversation*

In contrast to the simple mechanical transmitter-receiver model of the last section, Pask's conversation model involves participants in a conversation, at least one of which must be an autopoietic, self-organising system, that is, a system which, in response to perturbations and in the context of its purposive interaction with its environmental niche, constructs a reality for itself, i.e., it becomes 'in-formed' of its world. The important thing to appreciate is that, although the events that make up the conversation between the participants may appear to

49 For detailed (and classic) discussions of these issues see Cherry (1966) or Pierce (1980).

have code-like properties when viewed from an external observer's perspective, this is only ever partially so. Events provoke participants to construct meanings. As Heinz von Foerster puts it, "It is the receiver of a message who decides its meaning." Thus, Pask's conversation theory is concerned with the pragmatics of human communication and is consonant with the theories of Gregory Bateson (Bateson, 1972b, Watzlawick, Beavin, et al, 1968).

Pask begins his discussion of conversation with the model shown in figure 10. He refers to it as the 'skeleton of a conversation'. The model represents what Pask refers to as a 'strict conversation': where one participant, the learner, has agreed to learn about the topic expounded by the teacher. The conversation has a beginning (the learner or teacher asks a question) and an ending (the teacher deems that the learner now understands the topic). Of course, either party may end the conversation prematurely. In real life, conversations are potentially endless. They evolve: participants may adopt new roles and new topics for conversation may be invoked. The conversation itself may become a topic for conversation.

Rather than refer to codes or messages, Pask prefers to refer to the interactions between participants as 'provocations'. Provocations may be verbal, non-verbal or both. At a very general level, every provocation can be considered to be a command or invitation to the other to explain something or, if she cannot do that, to learn something.

Figure 10 shows a snapshot view of two participants in conversation about a topic. The horizontal connections represent the provocative exchanges. Pask argues that all such exchanges have, as a minimum, two logical levels. In the figure these are shown as the two levels: 'how' and 'why'. The 'how' level is concerned with descriptions of how to 'do' a topic: how to recognise it, construct it, maintain it, and so on; the 'why' level is concerned with explaining or justifying what a topic means in terms of other topics. These exchanges are 'provocative' in that they serve to provoke participants to construct understandings of each other's conceptions and (possibly) misconceptions of topics and the relations between them. This is the essential aspect that makes conversation theory constructivist and dialogical in approach and distinguishes it from other approaches that see teaching as the transmission of knowledge from teacher to learner. In the informal conversations of real life, participants move up and down logical levels in their interaction without necessarily being aware that this is happening.

The vertical connections represent causal connections with feedback, a hierarchy of cognitive processes that control or produce other cognitive processes. At the lowest level in the control hierarchy, there is a canonical world, a 'universe of discourse' or 'modelling facility', where the teacher (or computer-based

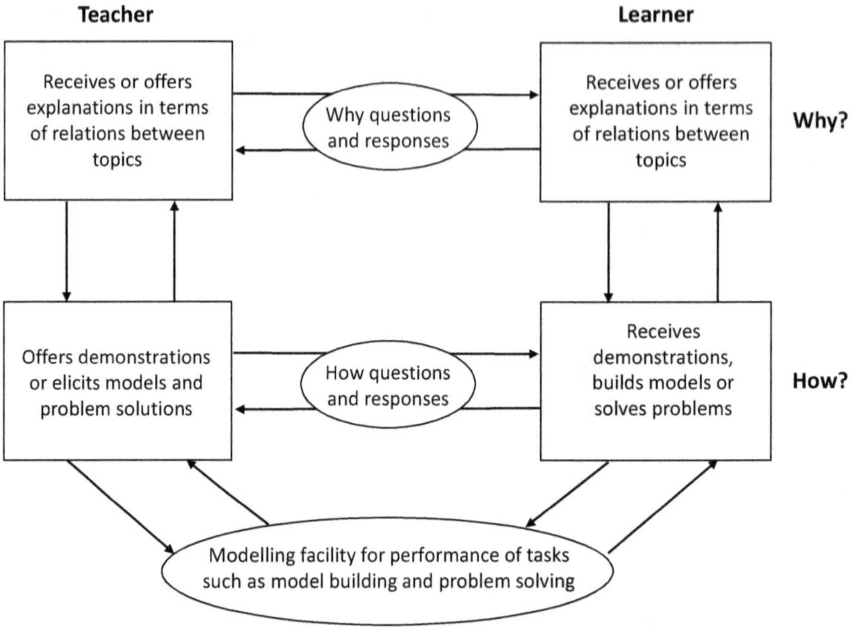

FIGURE 10 The "skeleton of a conversation": Pask's conversation theory (after Pask)

surrogate, as incorporated in CASTE, as described below) may instantiate or exemplify the topic by providing non-verbal demonstrations. Typically, such demonstrations are accompanied by an expository narrative about 'how' and 'why', the provocative interactions of questions and answers referred to above.

The form of what constitutes a canonical world for construction and demonstration may itself be a topic for negotiation and agreement. Examples of possible modelling facilities include pen and paper, the setting of a field trip, laboratories, and workshops.

Consider, for example, a set of well-defined topics in chemistry. A teacher may:
- model, demonstrate, or exemplify certain processes or events;
- offer explanations of why certain processes take place;
- request that a learner teaches back his or her conceptions of why certain things happen;
- offer verbal accounts of how to bring about certain events;
- ask a learner to provide such an account; and
- ask a learner to carry out experiments or other practical procedures pertaining to particular events or processes.

A learner may:
- request explanations of why;
- request accounts of how;

- request models, demonstrations, and examples;
- offer explanations of why for commentary;
- offer explanations of how for commentary; and
- carry out experiments and practical activities.

In turn, the learner uses the modelling facility to solve problems and carry out tasks set. He or she may also provide narrative commentary about 'how' and 'why'. In a computer-based environment, these may be elicited using computer-aided assessment tools with a variety of different question styles. The distinction between 'how' and 'why' allows for a formal definition of what it means to understand a topic. Understanding a topic means that the learner can provide both non-verbal demonstrations of 'how' and verbal explanations of 'why'. Asking the learner to do this is referred to as asking for 'teachback'.

Pask notes that, in principle, conversations may have many levels of interaction above the why level: levels at which conceptual justifications are themselves justified and where there is 'commentary about commentary'. Harri-Augstein and Thomas (1991) make this notion central in their work on 'self-organised learning', where the emphasis is on helping students 'learn to learn'. In brief, they propose that a 'full learning conversation' has three main components:

(1) conversation about the how and why of a topic, as in the basic Pask skeleton of a conversation model;
(2) conversation about the how of learning (for example, discussing study skills and reflecting on experiences as a learner); and
(3) conversation about purposes, the why of learning, where the emphasis is on encouraging personal autonomy and accepting responsibility for one's own learning.

Everyday conversations only approximate the form of the 'strict conversation' shown in figure 10. Participants do not regularly check their understandings by teachback, nor do they coherently justify, model, demonstrate or exemplify the topics they are discussing. Glanville (1997, 2001) has helped bring the skeleton of a conversation to life (to put flesh on its bones) and allow us to see how conversation theory captures the essence of what is happening when humans converse. Glanville emphasises the creativity and joyfulness that should, under ideal circumstances, accompany human conversation.

Glanville sets out a scheme that elaborates "the qualities necessary so that a conversation may function". Here, I outline Glanville's scheme with some additional commentaries of my own.

Glanville refers to two sets of requirements for a conversation to function, which he refers to as 'operational requirements', and 'inspirational requirements'. By the former, he means those aspects of the interaction process which must be present for the interaction to be considered to be a 'conversation', rather than a mere arbitrary or limited encounter between participants such as a simple exchange of greetings, goods, or physical contacts. One could perhaps also refer to them as 'functional' or 'processual' requirements. Inspirational requirements concern the attitudes and motivations that participants need to bring to the conversation for it to flourish as a mutually creative and uplifting encounter. Both sorts of requirements take the form of tacit, sometimes explicit, reciprocal expectations and are akin to the 'cooperative principle' of Paul Grice that states, "Make your contribution such as is required, at the stage at which it occurs, by the accepted purpose or direction of the talk exchange in which you are engaged" (Grice, 1975, p. 45).[50] Grice is concerned at a micro-level with 'good' (effective) practice concerning individual speech acts and responses and the implications ('conversational implicatures') that can be drawn from them. Glanville's requirements are concerned with the whole of the encounter that is the conversation.

Glanville's operational requirements[51]

1. A willingness to take part in a conversation about some topic. At least two participants are needed.
2. The topic around which the conversation takes place. The topic is negotiable and may change. There is an ever-present background topic, the reflexive topic, "What shall we talk about?"
3. The existence of different understandings of the topic in all participants. Without these differences, there would be no need for conversation.
4. Acts that are intended to present the form of these understandings so that the other participants can construct their understandings of these understandings together with acts that are intended to request the presentation of understandings (questions).
5. An ability to compare understandings: my understanding with my understanding of your understanding of my understanding and, vice versa, your understanding with your understanding of my understanding of your understanding. (In Pask's terms, this is part of the inner dialogue that informs conceptualisation.)
6. A logical structure of three co-located and contemporaneous levels: the level of the conversation, the subordinate level of the topic being

---

50 Grice goes on to state a set of maxims to be followed if the cooperative principle is accepted: Make your contribution as informative as is required (for the current purposes of the exchange). Do not make your contribution more informative than is required. Do not say what you believe to be false. Do not say that for which you lack adequate evidence. Avoid obscurity of expression. Avoid ambiguity. Be brief (avoid unnecessary prolixity). Be orderly.

51 For the sake of brevity, I have paraphrased Glanville's statements and omitted some of his elaborations. I have done this for both sets of requirements.

addressed, and the metalevel of error correction and topic modification (critique and evaluation of the conversation's progress).

7. An ability to monitor what is going on and to correct for incompatibilities between understandings by switching levels, i.e.:
   a. switching to a meta-conversation in which misunderstandings (temporarily) become the topic of the conversation
   b. switching back to the topic of the conversation itself. (Glanville notes that these switchings can occur recursively: misunderstandings may be misunderstood and require further error correction.)
8. A way of initiating and terminating the conversation. Glanville notes that in Pask's conversation theory, the occurrence of an understanding punctuates the conversation into discrete, possibly concurrent, episodes. In real life conversations, participants may terminate a conversation when mutual understanding is acknowledged, when there is an agreement to disagree, or as a matter of whim. Of course, the conversation may be taken up again on a future occasion. Glanville further notes that in real-life conversations, confirmation of mutual understandings is not expected for every communicative act. This is especially the case when participants believe that they already share many understandings. However, there is a price to pay for these shortcuts: the inadvertent pathologies of communication that occur when someone thinks someone else knows what is going on, when, in fact, they do not.[52]

Glanville's inspirational requirements

1. Recognition that the other has a different understanding.
2. Respect for this difference and the owner of the difference. Respect allows the participants to form their own individuality. Respect allows that I am not you.
3. Willingness to listen and to hear the other.
4. Willingness to construct my understanding of what the other presents to me as her understanding.
5. Willingness not to try to force my view on the other, i.e., not to exploit power relationships due to differences in social position.
6. An open mind, i.e., being prepared to give space to the other and to negotiate.
7. To regard surprises in the conversation not as threats but as being beneficial as opportunities to learn.
8. Willingness to change, develop, improve, i.e., to learn.

52 For a discussion of these pathologies and the forms they take in social organisations, see Scott (1997).

9. To recognise that what arises in conversation is not the property of a particular individual participant but rather is jointly owned. This is to recognise that the conversation has a life of its own. (In Pask's terms, the conversation itself is an embodied P-Individual).
10. A willingness to go with the conversation, to expect and allow for the unexpected.

Glanville argues that underlying these inspirational requirements are certain qualities that are associated with being a good and decent human being. These qualities are generosity, respect, honesty, a sense of drama, openness, imagination, acting on opportunities, and wit. He ascribes these qualities to his mentor, Gordon Pask, and goes on to say of his encounters with him:

> This is magic. Magic not as trickery or deceit, but magic in the unravelling enjoyment of mysteries and the growing and maintaining of wonder, a deep understanding of the miracle of our existing in our differing worlds and of their coming together in conversation through their beginnings and ends, of the poetic nature of our existence and of the unity of the void, the nothingness in and through which we dwell. And the love that is necessary that we can converse and interact with those others with whom we dwell, fairly, and doing justice to them and to ourselves.
>
> GLANVILLE, 2001, p. 667

4 *Human–Machine Interaction*

Conversation theory grew from Pask's interests in adaptive teaching systems.[53] He argued that the interaction between a learner and a teaching machine has the form of a conversation. The machine, as teacher, poses problems to the learner and learns about the learner to optimise learning. The learner attempts to solve problems and requests help and support. Pask noted that, for human–machine interaction in general, there are many contexts in which such interactions may be usefully considered to be conversational in form and for which the machine 'participant' may be explicitly designed to be a surrogate for a human conversational partner. Conversation theory provides the logic for how to design an effective machine participant.[54] Provocations need to take place

53 A non-technical account of the development of conversation theory can be found in Scott (1993). A discussion of conversation theory's relevance for educational technology can be found in Scott (2001).

54 Here, 'effective' means serving as a support for learning and problem solving and is to be contrasted with efforts to produce computer programs that can pass the Turing test (https://en.wikipedia.org/?title=Turing_test, accessed 19/06/2015).

via a suitable interface according to agreed semantic and syntactic rules. The pragmatics are provided by the role that the human participant has elected to play (learner, designer, game player) and are complemented by the affordances provided by the machine. In current parlance and practice, the latter is likely to be a computer-based application running various 'algorithms'[55] with access to the Internet (see below).

An early example is Pask and Scott's (1973) CASTE (Course Assembly System and Tutorial Environment). CASTE was developed in response to the need to provide learners with a description of a body of subject matter so that there could be a conversation between a computer-based tutorial system and the learner about topics being studied and about possible learning strategies. Pask often referred to CASTE as 'a vehicle for driving through knowledge'. Whalley (1995), with approval, refers to CASTE as a system that "provided both a 'virtual' environment for the student and a system to facilitate learning conversations about it" and "clearly worked as an integrated whole".[56] Using the conversational features of CASTE, system and learner agreed on what was likely to be an effective learning strategy and established an associated 'learning contract'. This latter typically included the agreement that progress was contingent on the student successfully 'teaching back' what he or she had learned so far. Using these contractual constraints, effective learning to 'mastery' level (Block, ed., 1971) was regularly achieved.

The main features of CASTE are shown in figure 11.

- An *entailment structure* for the whole of a course – a hierarchical form of concept map showing possible learning routes
- A modelling facility used for demonstrating topics and assessing understanding, following well-specified *task structures*
- BOSS (Belief and Opinion Sampling System) for sampling students' uncertainties about topic choices and topic content.
- A communications console affording different transaction types, e.g., 'state aim', 'select topic', 'elicit demonstration', 'submit explanation'.

After CASTE, Pask and colleagues developed 'Thoughtsticker', a sophisticated suite of programs that support knowledge elicitation and course design

55 "An algorithm (pronounced Al-go-rith-um) is a procedure or formula for solving a problem. The word derives from the name of the mathematician, Mohammed ibn-Musa al-Khwarizmi, who was part of the royal court in Baghdad and who lived from about 780 to 850. A computer program can be viewed as an elaborate algorithm. In mathematics and computer science, an algorithm usually means a procedure that solves a recurrent problem." http://whatis.techtarget.com/definition/algorithm (accessed 16/06/2015).

56 The technology that supported CASTE has been superseded many times, but the principles of its operation remain relevant (see Cong and Scott, 2017).

FIGURE 11 CASTE, main features

processes. (See Pangaro, 2001, for a very accessible account of Thoughtsticker functions). The key operation of Thoughtsticker is that of recommending novel perspectives and associated expository narratives. This is achieved by, first of all, eliciting from the user a 'knowledge fragment', a particular perspective and narrative form, and representing it as an entailment structure. Then, as a purely syntactic operation, Thoughtsticker adds links intended to turn the fragment into a cyclic 'mesh'. Novel perspectives are then generated by a 'pruning' operation, which removes redundant links. New perspectives are presented to the user as entailment structures that show alternative ways in which she might choose to expound the subject matter. The novel perspectives may provoke new insights and understandings. It is up to the user to accept, reject or modify the proposals.

In the larger domain of the Internet and hypertext knowledge archives, work inspired by conversation theory has been carried out on self-organising 'learning webs' where "Learning algorithms ... adapt the link strengths, based on the frequency with which links are selected by hypertext users ... to make the World-Wide-Web more intelligent, allowing it to self-organize and support inferences" (Heylighen, 2001) and on 'recommendation systems' (aka 'recommender systems') for "An extended process of information retrieval in distributed information systems" where "The knowledge stored in distributed information resources adapts to the evolving semantic expectations of their users as these select the information they desire in conversation with the information resources" (Rocha, 2001). A recommendation system is a generalisation of the Thoughtsticker course design tool. The system models the behaviour of the user of a set of distributed information resources, makes inferences about the predications she is using to give meaning to the information resources, and makes recommendations to the user based on those inferences. The user then may or may not validate those inferences by her acceptance or not of the recommendations. Thus a 'hermeneutic circle' is set up, where user and system may converge towards a mutually shared set of understandings.[57]

5 *Some Current Developments*

In 1993, inspired by the ideas of Pask, Vannevar Bush (1945) and Ted Nelson (1990), I set out the vision for a multimedia archive to support open learning, in which 'front end' systems interact conversationally with learners and teachers (see figure 12[58]). I later appreciated that the model I had constructed could be generalised to apply to the Internet, the World Wide Web, 'knowledge' archives such as Wikipedia, and the current developments that are seen as steps in the construction of a 'global brain', as first envisaged by H. G. Wells (1938).[59]

These steps include projects that aim to digitise all media objects (texts, images, sound and video files) and the creation of algorithms for systems

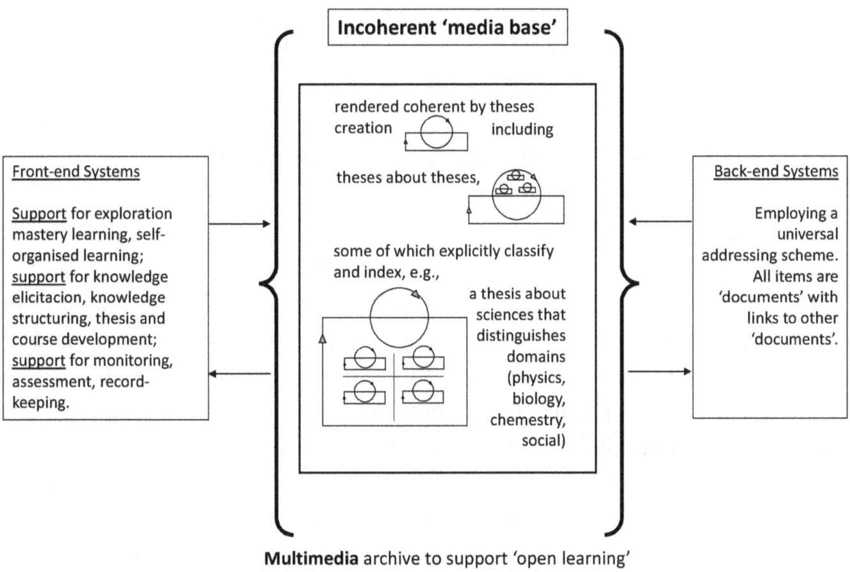

FIGURE 12 Towards a 'global brain' (from Scott, 1991)

57 For more, see https://en.wikipedia.org/?title=Recommender_system (accessed 18/06/2025).

58 In the figure, the arrowed circles represent a coherent thesis; the arrowed rectangles represent the pragmatic consequences of applying or holding the thesis to be true in a particular universe of discourse.

59 There is a useful discussion of different conceptions of a 'global brain' here https://en.wikipedia.org/wiki/Global_brain (accessed 18/06/2015).

that: search, data mine, translate, recommend, advise, analyse, filter, amplify, schedule, regulate, manage, connect, run intelligent tutoring systems, and abstract 'meaning' from corpuses of text using forms of 'cluster analysis' that tag key words, and the co-occurrence of words and phrases, to produce synopses. Robust and effective front-end conversational systems do not yet exist. We have the technology but, as yet, do not have the will and shared vision to create them.

6 *Concluding Comments*

Whether our context is global or local, technology mediated or face to face, we are continuously sending and receiving 'messages'. As Gregory Bateson (1972) puts it, as a participant in a social system, "One cannot not communicate." It behoves us, then, to take responsibility for the messages we 'transmit and receive'. What are our goals? How effective are we being in achieving them? With H. G. Wells[60] and many, many other great thinkers, I submit that education remains a priority. Too many minds are enchained by dogmatic belief systems. Too many of us have 'business as usual' attitudes and behaviours, in which the challenges of our times and the magic and mystery of being alive are trivialised.[61] I say more about these themes in later parts.

Part 6 Cybernetics and the Integration of the Disciplines

1 *Introduction*

Before it was named, the founding conception of cybernetics was that it should serve as a way of "integrating knowledge." In this part, the idea of integration (Latin, *integrare*, to make whole or make into one) is developed in three ways. First, there is integration through interdisciplinarity – the use of the 'language' of cybernetics (formal concepts and associated terminology) as a lingua franca to build bridges and facilitate communication between different knowledge domains (Latin, 'inter', between). Second, there is integration through transdisciplinarity (Latin, 'trans', across). Here, the models and terminology of cybernetics become systematized as a set of interrelated concepts, with cybernetics "having its own foundations" (Ashby, 1956, p. 1). With this

60 "Human history becomes more and more a race between education and catastrophe" (Wells, 1938).

61 I have discussed these themes in a number of publications. See, as examples, Scott (2009b, 2010, 2014).

conception, it is now possible for someone to be a 'cybernetician'. Cybernetics becomes a 'window on the world'. Wherever he looks, the cybernetician sees the ubiquitous phenomena of control and communication, learning and adaptation, self-organization, and evolution. His 'cybernetic spectacles' allow him to see any particular knowledge domain and the systems within it as special cases of abstract, general cybernetic forms. Third, there is integration through metadisciplinarity– in this application, cybernetics is a 'discipline about disciplines' (Greek 'meta', above). It comments on the forms and procedures that constitute particular disciplines as distinct knowledge domains. It sees the physicist as a builder of models, constrained by the properties of the domains and systems he distinguishes and interacts with. It sees the biologist the economist, the sociologist, the psychologist likewise. It comments on their activities as modellers, theorists, controllers, and predictors.

I begin with a discussion of 'coming to know' and 'knowledge sharing'. I then discuss particular knowledge domains. For reasons of space, coverage is selective. First, there is a discussion of the first order study of the domains of the natural sciences. The applied sciences, such as engineering, computer science, and the subdomains of robotics and artificial intelligence, whose relations to cybernetics are fairly self-evident, are not dealt with explicitly. There is then a more extended discussion of how cybernetics views the social sciences. This is followed by a brief discussion of the cybernetic perspective on the arts, humanities and vocational disciplines and the relation between cybernetics and philosophy.

2 *Cybernetic Epistemology*

As shown in figure 1, part 2, careful reading of Maturana, Von Foerster and Pask shows a circularity. The phenomenal domain of the observer may be taken as a starting point to account for the joint construction of the scientific domain. In turn, the 'scientific' may be taken as a starting point for an account of how observers evolve to become members of a community capable of constructing consensual domains. Although distinct knowledge domains do present problems particular to themselves, it is possible (and useful) to construct domain independent models of the processes of learning and 'coming to know' and the ways observers share understandings and do so in agreed ways. I first consider what is usually meant by the terms 'learning' and 'knowledge'. There is then a discussion of learning as a process of cognitive construction.

Learning, as biological adaptation, happens incidentally in the context of the pursuit of current need-satisfying goals. The process of adaptation is going on all the time. One cannot not learn. In humans, learning finds its highest expression. Our need to learn is so strong that, when there is little opportunity to learn, we experience boredom and actively seek out novel environments. Also, humans learn intentionally. We consciously set ourselves goals. We practise habits and skills. We reflect, conceptualise, and converse. We come together to learn and to teach.

When we learn, we are said to acquire 'knowledge'. There are many ways of classifying forms of knowledge. Following Bloom (1961), it is common practice to distinguish between 'knowledge', 'skills', and 'attitudes'. Often, different sub-types of 'knowledge' are distinguished. For example, Gagné, Briggs and Wagner distinguish motor skills, discriminations, intellectual skills, defined concepts, concrete concepts, cognitive strategies, attitudes, problem-solving, verbal information (names or labels, facts, knowledge), rules, and higher-order rules. Here, I avoid these more elaborate schemes for describing what is learned because the distinctions made are not always well-defined or easy to apply. I make use of one particular distinction, familiar from the time of Aristotle onwards, the distinction between 'knowing why' (cognitive, conceptual knowledge) and 'knowing how' (procedural, performance knowledge). (Answers to the questions who, 'what', 'where' and 'when' are subordinate questions, to be asked in the context of answers to 'how' and 'why'.)

Nicholas Rescher (1973, 1977), building on ideas taken from Piaget, has constructed a model of learning ('coming to know') in which two cycles of activity are distinguished: one corresponding to the acquisition and justification of 'why' knowledge, the other corresponding to the acquisition and consolidation of 'how' knowledge (see figure 13). Rescher uses this model in his discussion of how the scientific method has evolved to become the powerful tool that we know today. In the 'why' cycle, new conceptual knowledge is integrated with existing conceptual knowledge to form a coherent whole. In the 'how' cycle, new 'methods' (procedures, operations) are constructed and tried out and are subject to pragmatic correction. The two cycles, 'formal' and 'functional', interact: 'facts' may always be put into question; some form of constructive or operational/pragmatic 'proof' of theories and concepts may be asked for.

I also use the model in a more general sense to represent any belief system, where there is a body of knowledge (teachings, dogmas), and an associated body of practice, some of which, may make little use of logic and evidence. At the limit, 'knowing' may take the form of reciting set texts and of performing rituals, as in some kinds of cultish behaviour, or when military personnel are taught 'drills', such as the naming of parts of a weapon and being able to disassemble and assemble that weapon.[62] The reader may now see that Rescher's

62 In the film, *The Sand Pebbles*, the conceptual knowledge of the non-English speaking workers in the ship's engine room takes the form of a narrative about how to feed and

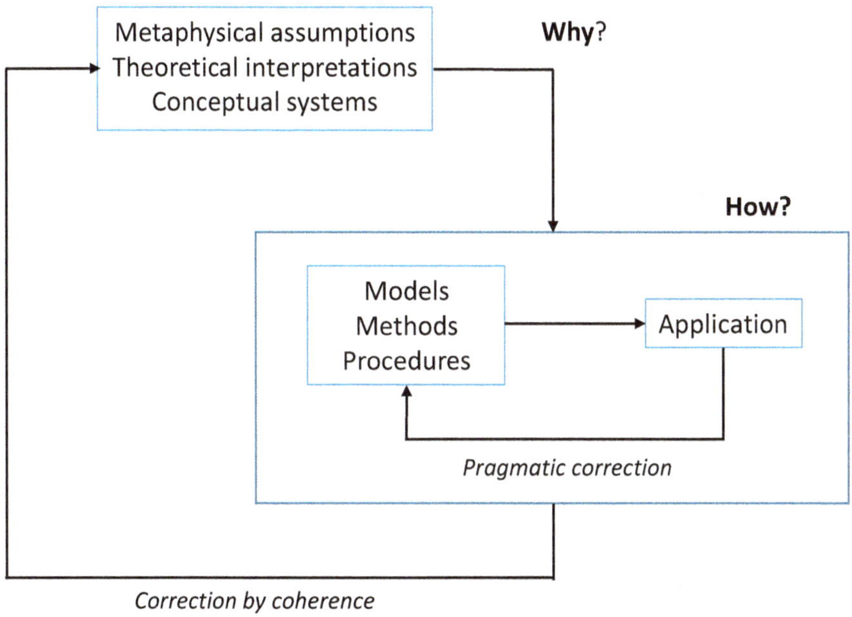

FIGURE 13 A two-cycle model of 'coming to know' (after Rescher)

model has essentially the same form as the model of a Pask P -Individual shown in figure 2 (part 3).

Generally, humans do not 'come to know' in isolation. What is needed is a theory of learning that includes the role of the teacher, where learner and teacher (in general, 'observers') are in conversation with one another. Pask's conversation theory, described in parts 3 and 5, serves this purpose. See, in particular, figure 9 in part 5.

3 *The First Order Study of Natural Systems*

As described by Karl Popper, Imre Lakatos, Frederick Suppe, and many others, the natural sciences have well-defined methodologies and procedures for justifying truth claims. A basic assumption of the natural sciences is that the observer is standing outside of an objective, subjectless universe. By Heisenberg's uncertainty principle, he cannot make an observation without affecting the system observed but, in all other respects, the events in the universe are independent of his thoughts and feelings. Such a universe is assumed to exhibit lawfulness. Events will always happen 'for a reason.' Miracles are not allowed.

look after 'the dragon'. The narrative guides their behaviour.

A domain of observation is distinguished and modelled as a set of variables, which together constitute a multi-dimensional universe of discourse. Particular systems are modelled as relations (products) and their transformations (processes). Values of variables are measured. Hypotheses are abduced about lawfulness within the domain and serve as the basis for the generation of testable predictions. Note how arbitrary are our knowledge domains and their names. Science is from the Latin word for knowledge (*scientia*); physics is from the Greek *physus* meaning nature; chemistry means 'mixing things' (Arabic *al kimiya*); algebra means 'concerning broken parts' (Arabic, *al jabr*); mathematics means 'that which is to be learned' (Greek, *mathema*); geometry means 'earth measurement' (Greek *geo metria*); biology is the study of life (Greek, *bios*, life); psychology is the study of the soul or the psyche (Greek, *psyche*).

There appears to be a general form to the processes of knowledge creation in science. Distinctions bifurcate and bifurcate as new concepts are articulated and discoveries made within domains until a point comes where there is a new synthesis that voids distinctions between domains, revealing new holistic constructs. As an example, the voiding of the distinction between the domains of magnetism and electricity gives the one domain of electromagnetism. Interdisciplinary studies are now commonplace, as in biochemistry and neuropsychology, where observations are made in more than one domain and where events at one level of discourse within a hierarchy of system types are used to explain events at the more macrolevel. Such approaches are only partly reductionist. It is now generally acknowledged, following Prigogine (1980) and others, that emergent systems have laws governing their behaviour at their own level, although remaining subject to the laws of lower level systems. Thus, chemical systems are emergents from physical systems; biological systems are emergents from chemical systems; psychosocial systems are emergents from biological systems. There are many classifications of systems types and accounts of their emergence and behaviour.[63]

From the perspective of cybernetics, the pursuit of 'a theory of everything' is just that, a pursuit, but without a final goal. As Spencer-Brown (1969, p. 106) puts it, "The universe must always expand to escape the telescopes through which, we who are it, are trying to capture it, which is us." With Prigogine's (op. cit.) thesis about the 'becoming' of the cosmos, there is a paradox of observation concerning our place as observers within a cosmos that is 'developing', 'becoming', 'evolving' or 'unfolding'. The observer is irrevocably a part of what

63 Pask (1979a) criticises what he calls 'systemic monism', the tendency of some theorists to treat all systems as just another system. As already mentioned, Pask finds it useful to make an analytic distinction between the 'biomechanical' and the 'psychosocial'.

he or she observes. She is ineluctably caught in a loop, where, as a 'being in time', she constructs concepts of 'being' and 'time'. But, although explaining has limits, cybernetics is also a praxis, an art, as quoted earlier: "L'art d'assurer l'efficacité de l'action" (Couffignal, op. cit.). We may still will and do.

4 *Approaches to the Study of Social Systems*

In this section, three approaches to the study of social systems are distinguished:
- first order studies of social systems and social behaviour;
- second order studies that investigate the interactions of social actors;
- approaches that distinguish social systems as autonomous wholes.

First order approaches to the study of social systems and social behaviour are those that adopt the modes of investigation of the natural sciences. The roots of this approach can be found in the empirical sociological studies of Emile Durkheim. We now have powerful methodologies to aid in this approach using systems dynamics modelling, agent based modelling and other computer simulation techniques.[64]

Second order approaches are those that investigate the interactions of social actors. What is of interest is not just the behaviour of the actors but, critically, the systems of belief (perspectives) that give meaning to their behaviours, including the beliefs (metaperspectives) they hold about each other's beliefs. The observer can no longer give himself the privilege of being an 'external observer' except by setting up elaborate contracts with participants (as in experimental psychology). He may form hypotheses about participants' beliefs based on observations of behaviour but may also give himself access to those beliefs by eavesdropping on or participating in conversational exchanges. The roots of this approach are many, including Max Weber's emphasis on the importance of 'verstehen' (understanding) in sociological research, Alfred Schutz's 'phenomenology of the social world' and the 'social behaviourism' of G. H. Mead.[65] Two related methodologies that come under this heading are 'action learning' and 'action research'. In both, the observer is a participant observer. She knows her interventions will change the system she is observing. Necessarily, she is a self-observer. She encourages other participants to become observers and self-observers, too. She aims to encourage the participants to learn how to self-organise in consensual and positive ways.[66]

64 For more about systems modelling and how to do it, see https://insightmaker.com/systemdynamics.

65 I particularly recommend the seminal discussion of what is peculiarly 'human' and 'social' by Peter Winch (1958).

66 For more about action learning, see Revans (1980). For more about action research, see Almaguer-Kalixto, Maass Moreno et al (2019).

Some approaches to the study of social systems are predicated on the idea that social systems are distinct forms of autonomous whole. That is, they are not just an observer's construct, as in the first order concept of system (above), they are characterized as being self-constructing and self-distinguishing. Early expressions of the idea of society as a 'functioning' whole that may be analysed into participating structures and processes are to be found in the writings of Karl Marx, Emile Durkheim and, later, in the theories of Talcott Parsons, who adopted ideas from cybernetics and systems theory in his theorising. Parsons' basic concept is that of an 'action system'. Action systems get things done; they reproduce society as an autonomous whole; they are functionally differentiated subsystems (for example the law, the economy, science) each with a medium or code which gives value to the actions they perform. As examples, the medium of law is 'power', the medium of business is 'money', the medium of science is 'truth'. Parsons emphasises that action systems are intrinsically social: they involve human communication as well as action; they are subordinate to the values of the culture in which they take place.

Niklas Luhmann, who studied with Parsons and was, for a while, 'Parsonian' in his thinking, went on to develop a theory of social systems, in which he abandons the concept of an action system in favour of the concept of a 'communication system'. Luhmann developed a theory of society, which he describes as a "far-reaching, elegant and economical instrument for explaining the positive and negative aspects of modern society." He also concedes that his theory is 'labyrinthine' (Luhmann, 1995).

Central in Luhmann's theory is his use of the concept of autopoiesis to characterize social systems. He begins by distinguishing several different kinds of autopoietic system: 'biological systems' are living systems; 'psychic systems' are 'centres of individual consciousness' which may play the role of 'persons' in particular social situations; 'social systems' are 'operationally closed', systems of 'communications'. His use of the term 'autopoiesis' for social systems has proved controversial.[67]

67 See the commentary by John Mingers (1994) and the critique by Randall Whitaker (2012). Whitaker is an acknowledged expert on the writings of Maturana and Varela. See his archive at http://www.enolagaia.com/AT.html (accessed 22/06/2020). Maturana and Varela (1980) use the term 'autopoiesis in the physical space' for living systems, which, *pace* Luhmann, implies a more general class of autopoietic systems, not just those found in 'physical spaces'. However, Maturana makes clear that in his conception of what is a social system it is not an autopoietic system (Maturana and Varela, op. cit., p. xxiv). Varela (1979) proposes the term 'organisationally closed' for the general class of system that the observer distinguishes as autonomous unities in the space in which they exist (see also footnote 14, p. 26). In later writings, to emphasise he is writing as a biologist/scientist, Maturana refers to the 'molecular autopoiesis' of living systems.

Luhmann goes on to distinguish three kinds of social system: 'interactions' in which persons encounter each other; 'organisations' which are associations of persons, as in clubs and business organizations; and, similar to Parsons, the 'functionally differentiated subsystems' of society, each of which has evolved a 'symbolically generalized communication medium'. Luhmann has added to the subsystems distinguished by Parsons and discussed their differentiation and 'interpenetration' in great detail.

Luhmann's, main aim is to construct a theory at the 'macrolevel', where social systems may be considered to have some kind of autonomy. To achieve his aim, Luhmann 'de-subjectivises' communication: he rejects the idea that a 'subject' must first consciously resolve to communicate in order to act communicatively. Rather, he asserts that communication is a supra-individual process. He captures this idea with the aphorism that "Only communication can communicate". Personally, I find fault with this in two ways: first, grammatically I cannot parse it; it seems to be a cross between an oxymoron and a tautology: human beings communicate, not 'communication'. Second, in communication studies, it is accepted that humans, who may be conscious of many things, unless asleep or dead, are not always conscious of the communicating they are part of. It is fair to say that Luhmann's theory of social systems is both complicated and complex. He has many followers who use his ideas selectively and in different ways. His ideas also have many critics. It is also fair to say that his ideas do not excite as much interest in the UK and the USA as they do in continental Europe and Japan.

A more important critique, from the perspective of seeking cybernetic transdisciplinary, clarity and unity, is Luhmann's distinguishing of 'psychic systems'. These are not well-defined as 'process/product' cybernetic models and serve to 'occultate' or obscure his aim of 'de-subjectivizing' communication.[68] Within his 'psychic' systems are rooted the notions of 'consciousness', 'meaning' and 'individuality', the very set of concepts that a science of the psychosocial should be elucidating. A satisfactory theory of the psychosocial, as in Pask's conversation theory, needs only to distinguish the biomechanical from the psychosocial. Luhmann's 'psychic systems' are redundant as a distinct category.

Thus, I argue that when Luhmann (1995, p. 271) writes, "Psychic and social systems cannot be reduced to each other ... they use different media of reproduction; consciousness and communication," he is plain wrong. Consciousness (knowing with oneself and with another) is communication; communication always implies some consciousness. There are many questions about the work

68 Luhmann's concept of a psychic system is taken from Freudian psychology. This is another borrowing from Parsons.

of both Parsons and Luhmann that continue to be debated; here are some examples. How useful is the concept of a functionally differentiated subsystem? Is Luhmann's approach truly superior to that of Parsons, if so, how? Do the function systems have some sort of independent 'reality' or are they just the constructions of an observer? What function systems can usefully be distinguished? Has the differentiation of the subsystems been inevitable in some way? How does the concept help in understanding cases where the subsystems are only partially differentiated, as in nation states where there is corruption and abuses of power?

Both Parsons and Luhmann discuss action and communication but define the function systems in different ways, making either action or communication central. From the perspective of 'meso' and 'micro-level' social science, I offer the following aphorisms: "In a social setting, to act is to communicate and to communicate is to act. One cannot not act; one cannot not communicate." There are other approaches to the study of social systems. I discuss these further in part 10.

5 *Cybernetics and the Arts, Humanities, and Vocational Disciplines*

As noted earlier, Louis Couffignal suggests that cybernetics may be considered to be an art, 'L'art d'assurer l'efficacite de l'action' (the art of assuring the efficacy of action). This suggests a useful perspective to adopt in order to gain cybernetic transdisciplinary insight into the nature of the arts, humanities and vocational disciplines. Quite straightforwardly, cybernetics is the art of designing and bringing about desirable artefacts and futures, but there are implications for what it means to act in the role of artist qua designer.[69]

In his discussions of ethics and second order cybernetics, von Foerster (1993) points out that we should accept responsibility for the worlds we have constructed and that this serves as a basis for an ethical approach to being in the world. Works of art – and here I include the discourses of scholars in the humanities – may provoke awareness, inform and enlighten, bring about the good. They may also corrupt, confuse, and limit the good.

Cybernetic maxims for effective action include von Foerster's, "A is better off when B is better off", "Act towards the future you desire" and "Act so as to maximize the alternatives." Pask advises that we may strive for 'unity without uniformity' and that, for the cybernetician, evil is that which limits the opportunities for actors to interact. These maxims may be helpful for fostering

69 See Pask's (1969b) seminal paper on "The architectural relevance of cybernetics".

reflective, ethical practice and 'learning communities' within the vocational disciplines (education, social work, governance, and related professions).

6 *Cybernetics and Philosophy*

The model in figure 13, above, is a cybernetic 'structural-functional-pragmatic' model of 'meaning' and 'truth.' It is structural in that it takes account of logical coherence within and between conceptual systems. It is functional in that it is based on the conception that living systems are autopoietic. It is pragmatic in that it acknowledges that the 'meaning' of terms and the 'truth' of theories are contingent not only on their logical coherence but also on the operational 'workability' of models, methods and procedures and the pragmatic consequences of action.

Although cybernetics is not committed to a particular metaphysics or ontology, it does acknowledge that there is a complementarity between 'knowing' and 'being.' As Wittgenstein puts it, "The world of a sad man is not the world of a happy man." What we know and believe affects how we experience ourselves to be. Our experiences affect our knowledge and beliefs, including our beliefs about what we may know and how we may be.

This part, so far, has attempted to give a cybernetician's view of what is 'knowing', what is 'knowledge' and to characterize domains of knowledge and action in an integrated way.

Whenever one abstracts from particular domains and systems to form general models, one runs the risk of being accused of oversimplifying or misrepresenting. I believe there is virtue in the transdisciplinary aims of cybernetics and that, although some abstractions may be quite simple, they may also serve as very powerful intellectual tools in their application. They may also have the beauty and elegance so often found when form is fitted to function. However, I am aware that there is much wealth in the details that have been suppressed in forming those abstractions. To construct broad brush stroke summaries of similarities and differences between domains of knowledge and the ideas and findings of great thinkers is one thing, to engage with those domains, in detail, is another. This latter activity may be enriching and enlightening despite or even because of disagreements about foundational framings and predications. However, for the cybernetician, learning is not just about mastering particular domains of knowledge and expertise, though this may be very useful and worthwhile. Critically, for the cyberneticians, learning is also about the second order processes of coming to know who we are and of sharing that knowledge. As Stafford Beer has put it, "The goal of a self-organising system is to learn to be what it is." In the next part, I say more about how cybernetics can be employed as an intellectual tool and as an aid for effective communication.

Part 7 In Defence of Pure Cybernetics

> Metaphysics is a subject much more curious than useful, the knowledge of which, like that of a sunken reef, serves chiefly to enable us to keep clear of it.
>
> CHARLES SANDERS PEIRCE, from his article "How to make our ideas clear" in HOOPES (1991, p. 179)

•••

> To seek out that which is not concealed is the self-confessed aim of our classic scientific tradition. Cybernetics, however, will only attain its true stature if it recognises itself as the science which reaches out for that which is hidden.
>
> GOTTHARD GUNTHER (1972, p. 33)[70]

•••

> We can no longer afford to be the knowing spectators at a global disaster. We must share what competence we have through communication and cooperation in working together through the problems of our time. This is the only way in which we can fulfil our social and individual responsibilities as cyberneticians who should practice what they preach.
>
> HEINZ VON FOERSTER (1972, p. 4)[71]

∴

70 Available here: http://www.vordenker.de/ggphilosophy/c_and_v.pdf Accessed 22/04/2018.

71 Available here: http://ada.evergreen.edu/~arunc/texts/cybernetics/heinz/competence/competence.pdf Accessed 13/09/2016.

1 *The Problem*

Cybernetics, as the science of control and communication, has a clear role to play in facilitating effective communication and identifying pathologies of communication in human systems (Scott, 1997). As a transdiscipline, cybernetics has a vital role to play in bringing sense and order to the emerging global conversation (Scott, 2010). In his book, *Ecological Communication*, Luhmann (1989) asserts that there is too much 'excitement' (noise and redundancy) in the marketplace of ideas and a lack of 'resonance' (harmony/compatibility) between humans and the biosphere of which they are a part. In this context, cybernetics can serve as a useful noise filter and variety attenuator.

These comments can be applied more generally to the political marketplace, where humans, using a variety of media, look for ideas worth 'buying into' and 'selling on'. Examples of this problem are many. In academia, there is a surfeit of publications and, to my eye, fewer and fewer scholarly safeguards concerning the quality of what is published, not least in the social sciences. Somewhat ironically, many publications debate this issue. For examples, see Ziman (2000) and O'Donnell (2019). Unfortunately, cybernetics, too, has become a victim of the academic excesses, giving the innocent reader less and less clarity about the discipline's aims and what it offers. This is a sad and tragic state of affairs given the many problems that humankind is currently facing. Here, I discuss the general question of how to think and communicate clearly, and how cybernetics can help. I also discuss, with examples, how this role for cybernetics may be obscured.

2 *Explanatory Schemas in Cybernetics*

Although it is possible from an historical perspective to discern the influence of cybernetics in biology, and the behavioural and social sciences, I think it is important to make these influences clear. To a large extent, scientists are quite uninformed of work in other disciplines, much of which may not be relevant for their interests. This is why the role of cybernetics as a unifying transdiscipline, discussed in the previous part, is so useful and important. Mutual ignorance of each other's work prevails between psychologists, sociologists and cultural anthropologists. There is also mutual ignorance between subdisciplines and between specialist lines of research within those subdisciplines Cybernetics can act as a filter for the bewildering variety generated by scientific research and scholarship. Isomorphisms and homomorphisms of formal concepts can be identified, as can redundancies of terminology. In other words, the major achievements of the early generations of cyberneticians in bringing unity and order to a wide range of disciplines need to be replicated. This calls for richer understandings of what cybernetics can contribute. Cybernetic understandings can help all scientists become more aware of their responsibilities. Cybernetics can also provide useful unifying syntheses of the biological, the psychological and the social.

I begin by reminding the reader of these two dictums from Humberto Maturana and Heinz von Foerster: "Anything said is said by an observer" and "Anything said is said to an observer" (von Foester, 2003, p. 283). Accordingly, cybernetics pays close attention to the pragmatics of conversation between human observers. Using Occam's razor,[72] with a careful analysis of the distinctions made, reveals the noise, redundancy and contradictions to be found in much academic discourse. To paraphrase Gordon Pask, the metaphors we humans manipulate, sometimes with cavalier abandon, need to be justified, to stand up to critical examination using logic and evidence. As pointed out by many, our use of language can entrap and confuse us in our rich use of metaphor (Lakoff and Johnson, 1980) and our proneness to faulty reasoning and logical fallacies. An example is assuming that anything that has a name must exist or have a definable 'essence' (variously called hypostatisation, reification, the fallacy of misplaced concreteness).

In the discussion of explanatory schemas in cybernetics that follows, the reader may find it helpful to recall Aristotle's doctrine of the four 'causes' (Greek, *aitia*, explanation; Latin, *causa*, reason for, cause)[73] needed in order to have knowledge of the world around us. In brief, the four 'causes' are 'material cause' (what a thing is made of), 'necessary cause' (what had to happen to bring the thing about), 'formal cause' (the form or idea of a thing), 'final cause' (the purpose to which a thing is put).

Erhardt von Demarus, in his (1967) thesis, "The Logical Structure of Mind", offers a variant on Aristotle's schema. He takes the concept of 'an occasion of experience' from the process philosophy of Alfred North Whitehead and applies it to the experience of an observer. For von Demarus, such an occasion of experience has four aspects: 'passage' in time, 'extension' in space, 'idea' (the forms distinguished by the observer), and 'intention' (the purpose of the observer). In similar spirit, Richard Jung in his (2007) book, *Experience and Action*, distinguishes four explanatory metaphors: two for *ens movens* (things that move or behave): and two for *ens volens* (things that show purpose). *Ens*

72 William of Occam (1287-1347) advises that one should not multiply entities or categories unnecessarily. See https://en.wikipedia.org/wiki/Occam%27s_razor (accessed 10/07/2020).

73 The translation of the Greek, *aitia*, as 'cause' is traditional in Western philosophy and, confusingly, is different from how the word 'cause' is used in everyday language, as in 'cause and effect', or to have a 'cause' to pursue.

movens are 'organisms' (which respond to stimuli) and 'machines' (which perform). *Ens volens* are 'mind' (intentions to act) and 'templates' (a 'semantic plexus', rules for conduct). We have already encountered Pask's analytic distinction between two types of organisationally closed system: biomechanical unities (which he refers to as 'Mechanical Individuals') and psychosocial unities (which he refers to as 'Psychological Individuals'). A social actor is a psychosocial unity embodied in one or more biomechanical unities.

These explanatory schemas are homomorphic and readily mapped onto each other (I leave that mapping as an exercise for the reader). The significance for cybernetics is that they make clear the richness of phenomena that the study of purposive systems must take into account, whether building purpose (anticipation, goal seeking, goal maintenance, adaptation) into mechanical systems or explaining and modelling purpose in biological, psychological and social systems. They show that first order and second order explanations are necessarily complementary.

3 *Obscuring Cybernetics*

Some combine cybernetics with other approaches and paradigms to construct what they argue are more complete or satisfying syntheses. I see this as unnecessary and, indeed, contrary to the role of cybernetics itself as a holistic, unifying transdiscipline. This practice also disregards Occam's razor and adds to the noise and excitement in the academic market place. Two examples of these practices are to be found in the social systems theory of Niklas Luhmann and the 'cybersemiotics' of Søren Brier.

Luhmann draws extensively on cybernetics, especially the work of von Foerster and Maturana.[74] However, he also incorporates ideas from traditions that are essentially alien to cybernetics, namely, Sigmund Freud's (1856–1939) 'depth' psychology (as already mentioned) and Edmund Husserl's (1859–1938) 'phenomenology'. He takes from Husserl's ideas in his use of the metaphors 'horizons of meaning' and 'meaning making'. In Scott (2012), I criticise Luhmann's theory of 'meaning making' for lacking a model. Much as I like Luhmann's insights about 'excitement' in the academic market place, I see him as guilty, like many others, of feeding that excitement, noise and redundancy by being so prolific in his writing.

Søren Brier and I have been friends for many years. I admire Brier as a most accomplished and creative historian and philosopher. In 2019, it became apparent that we have differing views about cybernetics: its form, content, role, and, in particular, how it relates to the work of C. S. Peirce (1839–1914). Søren invited

74 See, for example, Chapters 11 and 12 of his grand opus, *Social Systems*, (Luhmann, 1995).

me to set out my views, which I did in a short paper (Scott, 2019b). Here, I provide a brief reprise of how I see our differences.

My understanding is that Brier sees traditional cybernetics, in a narrow fashion, as being largely 'functionalist' and not addressing questions of meaning and subjective experience. Hence, he argues for the need for the augmentation of cybernetics by drawing on phenomenology (in the tradition of Husserl) and Peirce's 'semiotics'. Brier has created an all-encompassing metaphysical framework, 'cybersemiotics', that unites the natural sciences with the 'interpretive sciences' (by the latter, he appears to include both the social sciences and what others refer to as the 'humanities') (Brier, 2008). To meet this need, he draws extensively on Peirce's metaphysics, in which Peirce's semiotics plays a central part.[75] I see these moves as problematic.

Concerning Brier's first move, the augmentation of cybernetics with phenomenology and semiotics, I have already spoken about the alien nature of Husserl's phenomenology in my discussion of Luhmann's theorising. Concerning the role of semiotics, I differ from Brier in that I see Peirce as being a major influence in the development of cybernetics, including many aspects of his semiotics, and that, with a rich enough view of what cybernetics offers, Peirce's contributions can be readily assimilated. Certainly, concerning Peirce's metaphysical category of 'thirdness' (lawfulness, habit, representation)[76] in the world, I know of no thinkers who have characterised themselves as cyberneticians who do not have thirdness or some equivalent in their thought. All reject the reductionist materialism that has become the dominant paradigm in Western thought, academic and popular. At the risk of simplification, as examples, of purveyors of this latter paradigm, I cite Daniel Dennett, John Searle, Richard Dawkins, Stephen Pinker, Francis Crick and Roger Penrose.

Concerning Brier's second move, the construction of an all-encompassing metaphysical framework that unites the natural and the interpretive sciences,

---

75 Semiotics is the study of the role of verbal and non-verbal 'signs' in communication. Peirce classifies sign types, develops a formal logic of signs, and proposes theories of thinking, declaring that, "All thinking is in signs." There is now a wide field of scholarly endeavour that is covered by the labels, 'semiotics', 'semiology' and 'biosemiotics', which, because of the conceptual confusion and variety of views, greatly adds to the communication problems found in academic studies of communication. For some account of this wider field, see Cobley (ed.) (2001), Cobley and Jansz (2012).

76 C. S. Peirce makes a ternary distinction between fundamental categories: firstness, secondness and thirdness. In his writings, Peirce presents many definitions. In sum, firstness is where, as yet, no distinctions have been made; secondness refers to a world which exhibits causal dependencies (all causes lead to effects; all effects have causes); thirdness refers to a world which exhibits order (lawfulness, meaning). For a useful account of Peirce's three universal categories, see https://plato.stanford.edu/entries/peirce/#triad (accessed 25/06/2020).

I wish to note that there are what von Foerster refers to as 'undecidable questions' (von Foerster, 2003, pp. 291–295).[77] Metaphysics provides answers to such questions. However, their adoption as answers to the undecidable is a matter of personal predilection. There is the danger that the answers become dogmas and that those who adopt them become resistant (and, indeed, blind) to alternatives. It is vital that in a world that is ineffable and ineluctable, one can know when to agree to disagree.

There is much more I could say about the richness and intriguing nature of Peirce's thought but space is lacking. I would just like to raise three concerns. First, in my reading of Peirce (thus far), I have not found a coherent discussion in his accounts of 'signs' of the differences between animal and human cognition and communication. More fundamentally, I find the very concept of the 'sign' to be problematic. It is the receiver of a perturbation or 'irritation' (Peirce's term), animal or human, who pays attention to the event and finds it significant (meaningful, informative). Discussions of habitual ways of responding to events and of 'sign systems' are after-the-event attributions made by an external observer. As far as I know, Peirce did not deal with interpersonal perception and only briefly with developmental processes. There is now a rich literature on these topics, which are of interest to anyone (cybernetician, semiotician, linguist, social scientist, philosopher) studying human communication. I draw some of these threads together in Scott (2007) and Scott and Shurville (2011).

My second concern is that Peirce in his essay, "Man's glassy essence", on the dynamics of 'protoplasm' (Hoopes, 1991, pp. 220–229), comes close to the concept of a self-organising system but his formulation lacks the idea of organisational closure, i.e., that the system reproduces itself as an organisation. This concept is at most implicit. His ideas are a mix of bioenergetics, of abstractly formulated constraints found in his concept of 'habit taking', and of his monistic formulation of 'synechism' and 'hylozoism' (the continuity between the psychic – awareness – and dead matter, expressed in terms of the activity – or lack of it – of 'molecules'). To be fair to Peirce, he was writing some decades before the relation of the second law of thermodynamics to the question of what life is was set out by Erwin Schrödinger (Schrödinger, 1944) and before Heinz von Foerster, taking inspiration from Schrödinger, wrote his seminal paper "On self-organising systems and their environments" (von Foerster, 1960).

77 Here are some examples of undecideable questions: How did the world begin (cosmogony)? Is there a purpose to it all? What is life? Is there life after death? Do we have eternal souls? What happened before the big bang? Is there a God?

My third concern is with Peirce's concept of the triadic relation, sign, object and 'interpretant', where the interpretant is the 'thought' that relates an object and its sign. According to Peirce, that thought, in turn, becomes the object of a sign which is interpreted by the next thought. Thus, for Peirce, 'thinking' is conceived of as a linear concatenation of interpreted signs. This raises the question of when and why a line of thought ends. Peirce argues this happens when the initial 'irritation' is satisfied (the problem it poses is resolved). I suggest the reader compares Peirce's simple linear model with Pask's model of 'conceptualisation' as an organisationally closed system, in which a 'mesh' of concepts reproduces itself and evolves in response to both external perturbations and the internal variety generated by the dynamics of self-organisation (see also part 8).

4 *Enriching Cybernetics*

There is much other work, some of which predate cybernetics, that is largely compatible with cybernetics and can be readily assimilated into the cybernetics field. The developmental psychologist and epistemologist, Jean Piaget, is an early example. Piaget himself embraced cybernetics when it emerged. Other thinkers whose approaches are essentially cybernetic are found amongst psychologists, social psychologists, sociologists and cultural anthropologists who, like Piaget, have pragmatic, process-oriented understandings of how human development and learning is based on action, experience and social interaction. The list of such is long. Here are some examples of those who fit the bill quite well: William James, John Dewey, G. H. Mead, C. H. Cooley and Edward T. Hall.

Psychology as an empirical science embraces a wide range of methods and theories that take a 'phenomenological' approach, only some of which have a connection with the ideas of Edmund Husserl. There are overlaps with experiential psychology, humanistic (or whole person) psychology, all of which investigate the experiences and interpretations of human subjects. For now, it is sufficient to say that such studies can be carried on quite legitimately using cybernetic understandings of the human being as a unifying approach. There are many examples: the work of Pask and his colleagues in their studies of human learning; Piaget's and Lev Vygotsky's studies of child development; the work of the anthropologists Gregory Bateson and Roy Rappaport; the empirical studies of 'learning to learn' of Ranulph Glanville, and Laurie Thomas and Sheila Harri-Augstein. There is a very broad sense, in which almost all research labelled 'cognitive psychology' in the post-war years is cybernetic in orientation. This is because much of this work emerged as a direct result of the influence of cybernetics. (For an account of this, see Miller, Galanter, and Pribram, 1960.)[78]

5 *Cybernetics and the Communication Problem*

We need tools for clear thought, for example: Occam's razor, Spencer-Brown's (1969) logic of distinctions, the first order cybernetics of deterministic systems (Wiener, Ashby, Beer, Pask), Korzybski's (1933) 'general semantics', and the meta-philosophy of Wittgenstein (1953) and his characterisation of 'language games'.[79] Wittgenstein exercises Occam's razor in his recognition that philosophical problems are 'pseudo-problems'. With this statement, all philosophical distinctions such as mind/matter, self/world, free will/ determinism) are recognized by 'family resemblance' as being of the same category or class, addressing undecidable questions. Wittgenstein likens the resolution of these pseudo-problems to 'letting a fly escape from a bottle'.

Here, Peirce's ideas are very relevant. His view of how science works is, "The real, then, is that which, sooner or later, information and reasoning would finally result in, which is therefore independent of the vagaries of me and you. Thus, the very origin of the conception of reality shows that this conception essentially involves the notion of a community, without definite limits, and capable of an indefinite increase of knowledge," (from the article, "Some consequences of four incapacities" (Hoopes, 1991, p. 82)).[80]

Peirce invented pragmatism (which he renamed 'pragmaticism' to distinguish his ideas from what he considered to be less rigourous formulations). Pragmaticism is about achieving clarity of meaning in communication. "The whole function of thought is to produce habits of action. What a thing means is simply what habits it involves thus, we come down to what is tangible and practical, as the root of every real distinction of thought, no matter how subtle it may be; and there is no distinction of meaning so fine as to consist in anything but a possible difference of practice", from the article "How to make our ideas clear" (Hoopes, 1991, p. 168).

Pask's cybernetic conversation theory, with its account of forms of explanation, understanding, agreement, and agreement to disagree, lays a similar emphasis on the importance of clarity in communication. Pask does not draw

---

78 In Scott (2016), I argue that cybernetics can provide foundations and a unifying conceptual framework for psychology.

79 To show how the concept of a 'language game' can be fruitfully employed to clarify issues of communication, see Lyotard (1984).

80 Sørensen and Thellefsen (2009) provide a useful overview of Peirce's vision of how 'true scientists' pursue truth and meet their ethical obligations to the community of which they are a part.

directly on Peirce but he does draw on the broader pragmatic tradition found in American thought, notably, the work of Nicholas Rescher. In the 1970s, Pask and colleagues developed a rigourous methodology for knowledge and task analysis, which can be used by participants in conversation to express their beliefs and their understandings (Pask, 1975b, 1976; Pask, Kallikourdis and Scott, 1975). It is axiomatic in their approach that conceptual explanations should have a grounding in practice, in tasks that are performed (for example, by building a model or instantiating a concept by selecting from a set of alternatives).

Above all, we need to remind ourselves that, as insisted upon by Maturana and von Foerster, everything that is said is said by or to an observer. This means there is no authority or external reality that can be appealed to or hidden behind. As a participant in social interaction with other human beings (observers) one is asked to be present in the moment, to 'be here now', to be a cybernetician, and take responsibility for what one says and does. This requires, as far as possible, constant monitoring of what one is saying and doing and why one is saying and doing it.

Part 8 Sociocybernetic Understandings of Consciousness

> Everything is in interaction and reciprocal.
>
> ALEXANDER VON HUMBOLDT (1769–1859), cited in WULF, *The Invention of Nature* (2015, p. 59)

∴

1 *Introduction*

This part aims to show how, using abstract concepts from cybernetics, one can combine biological, psychological and sociological concepts to provide conceptual clarification and insightful understandings of human consciousness. The part is structured as follows. There is a brief discussion of how the term 'consciousness' is used and abused in contemporary neuroscience and cognitive science (philosophy of mind, cognitive psychology, and artificial intelligence). As a preface to a cybernetic approach to this topic, there is a brief discussion of reflexive cosmogony and process metaphysics. This is followed by a cybernetic characterisation of awareness and consciousness. Some models of conscious systems are then presented and discussed. There is then a discussion of how cybernetic understandings of consciousness can give ethical guidance for how to characterise, create and sustain communities in which goodwill prevails.

2 *Use of the Term 'Consciousness'*

In neuroscience and cognitive science, 'consciousness' is frequently treated as a kind of 'essence' found in subjective experience. Explaining how this essence arises – or may arise – in natural and artificial systems is referred to as the 'hard problem of consciousness'. This approach may be seen as dualistic in that an ontological distinction is made between the world of experience (mind, subjectivity, 'qualia'[81]) and the world of matter (brain and body). A search is then made in the brain/body system for that which gives rise to subjective experience. In contrast, in cybernetics, and its precursors in American pragmatist psychology (for example, in William James' *Principles of Psychology*, first published in 1898), it is assumed that for all subjective experience there is a material (brain/body) correlate, captured in the aphorism, "A thought in the head is like a fist in the hand." Wittgenstein argues that it is our use of language that leads us to believe there is an inner world of thoughts and feelings separate from the behaviour of the brain/body system.[82]

Here, following the usage by cyberneticians (McCulloch, von Foerster, Pask, Jung), I use the term 'consciousness' to refer to 'knowing with', where the knowing can be with another or with oneself (Latin, *con-scire*, to know with). This usage distinguishes consciousness, as a primarily human phenomenon, from the more general phenomenon of 'awareness' (wakefulness) observed, to some degree, in all living systems. With consciousness, there is a shared awareness. It is also fair to admit that, to a limited extent, there may be shared awareness between humans and other species and within and between other species. Pask presents a cybernetic account of awareness. Awareness is characterised as a product of the dynamics of a self-organising, autopoietic system. Such systems are energetically open (they metabolise foodstuffs to maintain themselves as material beings) and may have an excess of energy available ('free energy') which allows them to be active 'eaters of variety'. That is, in waking states, they seek novelty by monitoring, exploring and enlarging their environmental niches. There is an ongoing process of variety (uncertainty) reduction, as they learn to anticipate and control their environments, accompanied by variety (uncertainty) generation as they continue to explore

81 Qualia are particular subjective experiences, such as a pain, a taste, or the experience of a colour. The singular is a 'quale' (first used by C. S. Peirce).

82 See Hacker (1997) for a succinct summary of Wittgenstein's arguments. See Hacker (2012) for a Wittgensteinian critique of how the term consciousness is used in the neuroscience and cognitive science communities.

their environment. When fatigued, they rest and renew themselves. These processes can be found, to some degree, in all living systems (Pask, 1968, p. 1).[83] This thesis is the cornerstone of Pask's work on adaptive teaching machines, in which the machine optimises the rate of learning of the student by presenting problems of increasing or decreasing difficulty to avoid the student being bored, overloaded or fatigued.

Awareness of self as a self, 'self-consciousness', appears to be an achievement of humans only, linked to their use of language and their development as social beings within a community. Mead's (1934) analysis of the genesis of self and society is now classic. According to Mead, the 'I' emerges in the dialectic of reciprocal role-taking: taking the other's perspective. Thought becomes an inner dialogue between perspectives: the self is a social process. 'Self-image' is a social construct and may take different forms in different cultures.[84] In Pask's terms, a 'self' is a conversational process embedded in a conversational process (society, culture). Berger and Luckman (1967), drawing from Mead's thought, tersely capture the essence of the self/society dialectic as follows. Through social interaction, action is 'objectified' as social institutions, shared rules, roles, attitudes and perspectives. A child born into a given culture encounters the 'social objects' and internalises them as concepts (eigenbehaviours). Creatively, humans constitute novel social institutions and succeeding generations are made to fit and conform. The most powerful social object is language itself. It is a system of rules, roles and attitudes in its own right and is a major means of access to other social objects. In Piaget's (1952) account, as language is acquired it makes available its 'cognitive instruments' for the service of thought. At the same time, it shapes thought. As the infant grows into language, the power of language to describe, coordinate and calculate is revealed. The necessary underlying cognitive structures (concepts, eigenbehaviours) evolve, through action and experience, to fit the template of language. In turn, language evolves to capture new forms of cognition and affect.

3 *Reflexive Cosmogony and Process Metaphysics*

> The world … is constructed in order to know itself … Whatever it sees is only partially itself.
>
> GEORGE SPENCER-BROWN, *Laws of Form*, p. 105

83 A most excellent example is to be found in the behaviour of a human infant.

84 For more about the development of self-consciousness, see Maturana (1995), Scott (2007) and Scott (2011b). See also the entry on 'interaction' in part 4.

...

To know not knowing, sublime; to not know not knowing, faulty.
TAO TE CHING (my translation)

∴

I begin this section with the above quotations to emphasise that we humans are a mystery that is part of a mystery. We are faced with undecidable questions (von Foerster, 2003, pp. 292–293). As human beings, our ultimate freedom resides in how we choose to answer such questions. Our answers about our world take the form of stories we tell ourselves, cosmogonies. Insofar as these stories address questions about who, what and why we are, they are reflexive cosmogonies. Where should our stories begin? Answering this question takes us into the realm of metaphysics. Here are some examples of metaphysical starting points.

Carl Jung (1916) begins with a distinction between *Pleroma* (formless 'stuff') and *Creatura* (the world of distinctions). Jung is cited by Gregory Bateson in his discussion of 'form, substance and difference' (Bateson, 1972a); in Hindu philosophy one finds a distinction between the *Void* (full emptiness) and the *Not-Void* (empty fullness); Richard Jung (2007) begins his narrative with a distinction between *Indefiniteness* and *Form*; George Spencer-Brown (1969) distinguishes the *void* from the *form of distinction*. Essentially, these binary distinctions are saying the same thing: there is the world of undifferentiated, undescribable, limitless all; there is the world of distinction and description constructed by observers. As mentioned in the previous part, C. S. Peirce distinguishes three fundamental categories: *firstness*, *secondness* and *thirdness*. Firstness is where, as yet, no distinctions have been made; *secondness* refers to cause and effect dependencies; *thirdness* refers to order (lawfulness, meaning).

From classical times, a distinction has been made between cosmogonies that emphasise what the world is made of (its being) as ultimate, unchanging essence or substance and those that emphasise the processes of change (the world's becoming) as the only constant. Cybernetic theories are oriented towards process, how things behave, and look for explanation, not in what those things are made of, but in how they are organised. Aristotle, often cited as the 'father of biology' as well as the 'father of logic', has also been claimed (by Gregory Bateson amongst others) as the 'father of cybernetics'.

I referred to Aristotle's doctrine of the four 'causes' in the previous part. Aristotle also distinguishes three types of 'psyche' (usually translated as 'soul' or 'mind') of increasing complexity: the psyches of plants (the 'nutritive soul), which give them the ability to grow and reproduce; the psyches of animals (the 'sensible soul'), which give them the abilities of plants and also the ability to perceive and move; and the psyches of humans, which give them the abilities of animals and also the ability to reason. In cybernetic terms, the different psyches are different forms of organisation, where the human ability to reason is intrinsically bound up with the use of language.

Apropos of our interest in conscious systems, those with which the observer may converse, it is useful to note Pask's (1969) distinction between taciturn systems and language-oriented systems. Taciturn systems are distinguished and observed by an external observer who infers or builds in their goals. Language oriented systems are self-distinguishing and set their own goals. They are interacted with (conversed with) by a participant observer. Aspects of Pask's distinction were later summed up by von Foerster in his distinction between first and second order cybernetics (von Forester, 2003, pp. 285–286). To attempt to model and understand conscious systems (observers) is to study language-oriented systems and to engage in second order cybernetics.

4 *Cybernetic Models of Learning in Conscious Systems*

Cybernetic models help us understand how the brain/body system functions as a complex command and control system. Classic examples include: Ross Ashby's (1948) work on 'ultrastability' (the brain's ability to adapt to perturbations), as part of which he built a hardware model, the 'homeostat'; Kilmer, McCulloch et al.'s (1969) use of computer simulations in their studies of the brain's reticular formation and it's ability, as a heterarchical control system, to make virtually instantaneous decisions about what 'mode' to put the body in (fight, flee, eat, sleep and so on); Maturana's (1970) descriptive model of the nervous system as an operationally closed network; and von Foerster's (2003) many different models (mathematical, diagrammatic) of how the brain constructs a stable 'reality'.

In the theorising that follows, I make an analytic distinction between organisationally closed (autopoietic) bio-mechanical unities, which exhibit passage and extension, and organisationally closed psychosocial systemic unities, which exhibit idea and intention (Pask's M-Individuals and P-Individuals, respectively). I describe two models, a diagrammatic model and a computer program simulation model.

The model in figure 14 is similar in appearance to many models to be found in cognitive psychology that show 'memory' as a series of separate stages, involving 'storage and retrieval'. However, the model in figure 14 is different in several ways. Rather than showing a series of relatively static stages, I attempt to show the complex dynamic processes that occur as a human learns. The learner's brain/body system is a biomechanical unity that actively seeks and processes variety, and which embodies the psychosocial unity as an ongoing process of conceptualisation. As an embodied psychosocial unity (P-Individual), the learner may set her own goals and direct her own attention. As the brain/body system adapts and habituates to the events captured by the sensory systems, it seeks more variety in accordance with any goals that have been consciously set. Several bodily processes guide and affect the systems. In figure 14, these are labelled: kinaesthesia (having as subsystems the proprioceptive and vestibular systems); interoception (sensing of the body's internal state); algedonic (pain, pleasure) feedback; and the endocrine and immune systems which affect the overall functioning of the brain. There is also feedback through the environment: motor responses affect sensory inputs, which inform the learner about where she is and what is happening around her. Familiar settings call forth learned responses. Unfamiliar settings induce learning and adaptation that reduce uncertainty. The figure shows the parts of the system where there is awareness, where the learner is conscious with herself of what is happening. The blue lines show the routes through the system, from sensing to responding. The black lines show the feedback paths. The red line indicates the feedback through the environment, from responding to sensing. The term 'external storage of information' refers to the ways in which previously acquired knowledge (concepts, eigenbehaviours) are brought into play in familiar situations. In response to the setting, the brain reconfigures itself and the relevant concepts are reconstructed. As an example, the learner remembers the details of how to drive a car when she is sitting in the car. Away from the car, she may only have a partial recollection of what is required.

The second model is a computer program that simulates the acquisition of a keyboard skill. As a graduate researcher, under the supervision of Gordon Pask, I carried out a series of experimental studies of subjects learning to type. Learners followed different regimes. In control groups, subjects followed conventional drill and practice methods. In experimental groups, subjects were taught using adaptive teaching machines that presented stimuli, indicating which keys to press, at rates which were adapted to the learner's degree of success. As part of these studies, in 1975, I constructed a computer program model that helps explain how learning takes place. As an aid to exposition, the model had several versions of increasing complexity. The most complex model was called the "Full Typist" model. Here I give a brief description of how the model works. For more about the Typist models and the experimental studies on which they were based, see Scott and Bansal (2013, 2014). For the most detailed account, see Scott (1976).

The Full Typist model simulates the acquisition of the skill of touch typing. It explains why proficient touch typists lose access to a conscious knowledge of the structure of the skill, and why they are frequently aware that an error has been made, before the receipt of any external feedback. These phenomena can be observed in the acquisition of all perceptual-motor skills. The typist is modelled as a dynamic self-organising system, in which achievement of goals is subject to a 'free energy' economy. A simulated 'teaching system', presents individual letters (the keyboard characters) as a series of discrete events, referred to as 'experimental trials'. For each trial, the learner has a limited time in which to respond with a key press; this is simulated in the model by there being a fixed amount of energy available for each trial. In both cases, the 'teacher' provides feedback about whether or not the response was successful. Learning is simulated as an evolutionary process. There is an initial population of possible TOTE unit[85] response 'operators'. Some operators move a particular finger; other operators decide the direction in which to move that finger. The Typist model begins by randomly selecting operators at each trial, first a finger operator and then a move operator. Successful operators are retained, ready for use for the next time that that letter appears; unsuccessful operators are discarded. If energy is available, 'complex operators', which are a combination of a successful finger operator with a successful move operator, may be constructed. There is an advantage to doing this because applying a complex operator takes less energy than applying simpler operators separately. As successful operators are constructed, energy becomes available allowing the model to use 'logical operators' (inference rules), which use knowledge of the keyboard layout, the position of keys relative to each other, to help select the operators which are likely to be successful, thus reducing the set of possible responses. For example, if a particular 'move' + 'finger' combination is known to be a successful response to a particular stimulus, that selection can be ruled out for other stimuli. In a human typist, cognitive processes may be applied concurrently and may interact, speeding up the logical search for an appropriate response. In the model, the interaction of operators applied concurrently is simulated by a set of serial executions of the logical operators that exhausts the set of possible interactions.

Over time, the typist achieves proficient and energy-efficient operation, and conscious knowledge of the keyboard is lost. She is free to think of other things.

85 For a description of a TOTE unit, see the entry 'process and product' in part 4.

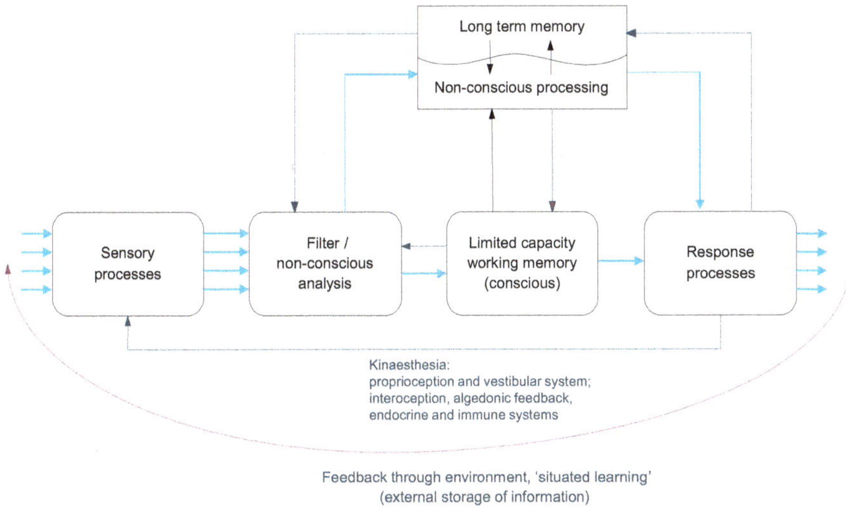

FIGURE 14 The dynamics of learning and awareness

In the model, proficient performance is characterised by the state of affairs where 'which finger in which direction' operators are immediately available and applied. The knowledge of the keyboard now serves as an internal check that confirms or disconfirms what was done. If there is confirmation, typing continues. With a disconfirmation, typing is interrupted; the unsuccessful operator is discarded and the typist becomes aware of having made an error.

The theoretical justification for the form of the simulation is that the cognition of the proficient typist is seen as a unitary organisation in which particular processes, when they do not conflict, go on concurrently, autonomously and unconsciously. When there is conflict, there is uncertainty; the typist becomes aware that something requires her attention. and she is called upon to attend consciously to the task at hand. The uncertainty is reduced when the typist decides how to resolve the conflict.

5 *Generalising the Typist Model*

The Typist model can be generalised for domains other than touch typing as follows. In the model, there are operators that bring about finger movements for key pressing. In general, there are cognitive processes that bring about or maintain a relation in a particular universe of interpretation. In previous parts, following Pask, we have referred to these as 'concepts'. Also, in the model, there are processes that construct, select and maintain the movement operators. In general, there are cognitive processes that bring about or maintain concepts. In previous parts, we referred to these as 'concepts of concepts'. In the Typist model, the overall process of acquiring and performing the skill has a cyclic form: knowing leads to doing which leads to further knowing and further doing. The process is a whole that reproduces itself in the setting of touch typing. In general, there are organisationally-closed systems of concepts that reproduce themselves in a variety of settings (referred to by Pask as 'conversational domains'). In previous parts, we have referred to these systems as embodied P-Individuals (psychosocial unities) (see figure 2).

The above models explain key aspects of human cognition: how human beings learn about their world, how consciously constructed knowledge becomes proceduralised (automatic), how conflict in concurrently executed processes may engender the conscious awareness of error and uncertainty. The models offer first order explanations of observed systems. They also offer second order explanations of observing systems: they explain the observer to herself. As the constructor of the models and narrator of the theories that give them significance, I am aware I have been engaged in learning and remembering: acquiring new knowledge and new skills and remembering (reconstructing) old knowledge and old skills. The theories are specialist topics within Pask's conversation theory. As such, they provide an account of their genesis. One's intention to solve a problem and one's understanding of relevant principles serve as constraints to which evolving concepts must fit. The construction of a satisfactory new concept may happen within a few milliseconds or may require deep thought and gestation over days, weeks or a lifetime.

6 *Creating and Maintaining Healthy Communities*

> Speech has enabled ... us to conquer every square inch of land, subjugate every creature ... and (enabled) the creation of an internal self ...
>
> TOM WOLFE, *The Kingdom of Speech* (2016), p.165

•••

> With our growing self-consciousness and increasing intelligence we must begin to control tradition and assume a critical attitude toward it, if human relations are ever to change for the better.
>
> ALBERT EINSTEIN (1946)

∵

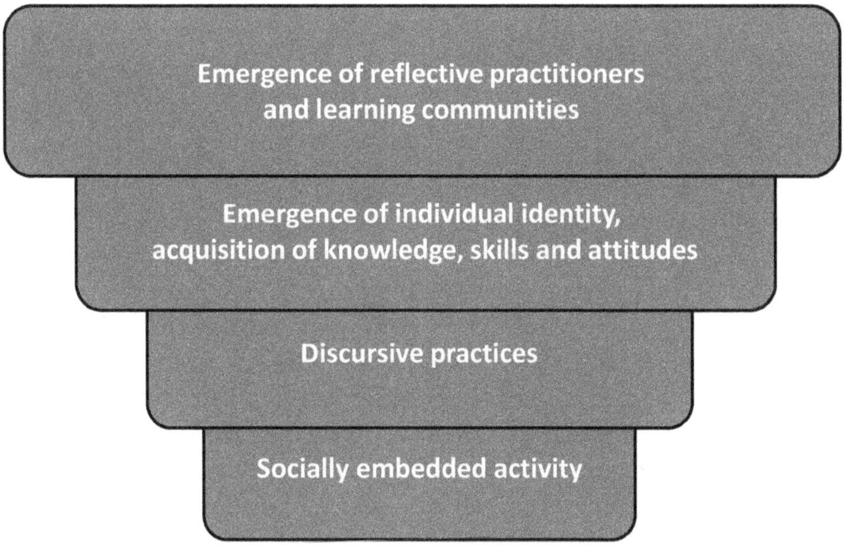

FIGURE 15 Learning, as communities, to do things better

I have said something about how consciousness arises and how selves are formed in child development and I have briefly discussed the central role of language in these processes. I sum up my thinking in figure 15.

There, I include my concern with how, if we understand the processes in question, we may cultivate communities and societies that exhibit the best practices of creative and harmonious living (and what I have referred to in part 2 as 'cybernetic enlightenment'), beginning with socially embedded activities (working, playing, learning, teaching and child-rearing) and the conversations that arise in them.

Part 9 Reflections on the Sociocybernetics of Social Networks[86]

1 *Introduction*

> No man is an island, entire unto himself.
>
> JOHN DONNE

•••

86 This part is an abbreviated version of Scott (2018b).

We are all connected.

Ephesians, 4, 25

∴

This part uses concepts from sociocybernetics to explore how the term 'social network' is used. I begin with an overview of what has become known as 'network science' and continue by asking what is 'social' about a social network. I go on to consider the various forms that social networks may take. I then discuss the theoretical question: what distinction is there, if any, between a 'social network' and a 'social system'? Next, I provide a brief critique of 'connectivity theory' and 'Actor-Network-Theory'. Finally, I comment on the emerging 'global conversation'.

2 *Network Science*

Network science is the name given to work on complex systems in which system structure and behaviour are modelled as networks (Barabas and Frangos, 2014). A network consists of a set of nodes (also known as 'vertices' or 'points') connected by links (also known as 'edges', 'arcs' or 'ties'). The nodes represent system components. The links represent specific relationships between those components. Interestingly, formal approaches to mapping relationships between social entities first emerged in the social sciences as 'sociometry'. Jacob Moreno (1934) constructed networks showing interpersonal relations. He referred to these as 'sociograms'. In later work, the mathematician, Frank Harary, and the sociologist, Dorwin Cartwright, applied 'graph theory',[87] to the study of social relations and, with Robert Norman, published a seminal text on graph theory (Harary, Norman et al., 1965). Graph theory provides the theoretical underpinning for network science and its many applications in physics, computer science, engineering, biology and the social sciences. Network science is also used as a tool in the broad field of 'data visualisation' (see Rosling[88]), geographic information systems and studies of internet

87 In mathematics, the formal study of 'graphs', networks of vertices and edges. See https://en.wikipedia.org/wiki/Graph_theory (accessed 16/09/2015).

88 Hans Rosling (2006). "The best stats you've ever seen". TED talk, http://www.ted.com/talks/hans_rosling_shows_the_best_stats_you_ve_ever_seen?language=en (accessed 10/09/2015).

connectivity. In a study, of interest to sociocybernetics, Glattfelder[89] has used network theory to study ownership relations. Network theory also plays a central role in the work of Alex Pentiland (2014) on 'social physics'.

3 *What Is 'Social' about a Social Network?*

A social network is a network in which the nodes are social actors (individuals or organisations) and where the links represent aspects of social relationships, for example, who knows whom, who visits whom, who is related to whom, who works for whom, who communicates with whom. The essential feature that makes the network 'social' rather than 'physical' or 'biological' is the reciprocity of relations between social actors and the expectations that underpin them. Social actors think about each other and know that this is the case.

Using the terminology of Pask's conversation theory, as used in preceding parts, a social actor is a P-Individual (psychosocial unity) embodied in one or more M-Individuals (biomechanical unities), capable of conversing with other social actors and of self-reflection (conversation with herself). A social actor may be an individual human being or a collective of some kind, whose embodiment is distributed over two or more M-Individuals. A typical M-Individual is the brain/body system of a human individual and its extensions that add to the functionality of the M-Individual. Examples of extensions include writing instruments, clothing, vehicles, aids for vision and hearing, and aids for computation and communication. For the latter, there are several developments, including: the aim to digitise all media objects (texts, images, sound and video files); the creation of algorithms for systems that search, data mine, translate, recommend, advise, analyse, filter, amplify, schedule, regulate, manage and connect. There is also the potential for tools such as search engines to be equipped with artificial intelligence and interaction protocols that would allow them to engage with users as surrogate participants in a conversation. (This possibility is discussed in part 5.)

It would be remiss of me not to mention the 'political' aspects of the use of social media and related technologies. These are aspects of these systems that it behoves users to be aware of, and to reflect on the implications for social empowerment, privacy and social control. These topics continue to be debated.[90] To deal with them in detail is beyond the scope of this part.

---

89 J. B. Glattfelder (2013). "Who controls the world?" TED talk, http://www.ted.com/talks/james_b_glattfelder_who_controls_the_world?language=en. (accessed 10/09/2015.

90 An important contributor is the World Wide Web Foundation, headed by Sir Tim Berners-Lee. http://webfoundation.org/ (accessed 19/09/15).

Certainly worth mentioning are the tensions between issues of state and organisational security, and personal freedom. There are also complex issues of ownership of data that are particularly pertinent in a context where data in digital form may have very long lifetimes.

4 *The Forms That Social Networks May Take*

An external observer typically uses nodes to represent members of a social network and links to represent their 'connections' or 'interactions'. The questions that then arise are (i) what qualifies an actor to be a member of the network (ii) what cognitive, affective and instrumental capabilities are attributed to such an actor (iii) what kind of connection or interaction do the links represent (iv) what other properties or constraints are attributed to the network as a whole (v) what relations exist between networks, as perceived by an external observer or by the members of those networks.

Concerning (i), membership of a network may be something that the members attribute to themselves, consciously, or it may be something that the external observer attributes to them. Concerning (ii), by Occam's razor, the external observer need only attribute those capabilities that are relevant for the hypotheses that are guiding his investigations. For example, the cognitive capability of distinguishing between alternatives, the affective capability of placing value on alternatives, the instrumental capability of sending and receiving messages using different means. Concerning (iii), the links may be unidirectional or bidirectional, representing the possibility of sending or receiving messages to or from a particular other member and of the existence of one or more shared attributes that relate the members in question. Concerning (iv), the network may be considered to be 'closed', i.e., no new members may be added or new members may be added only if they meet certain criteria, or 'open', i.e., membership is unrestricted, except with respect to possession of relevant capabilities. If closed, it may be partially or fully 'saturated', i.e., a fully saturated network is one in which every member is directly connected to every other member. Membership of a network may also be 'voluntary' or 'involuntary'. It is also worthwhile to make a distinction between networks where membership is 'tacit' or taken for granted, i.e., not consciously reflected upon, and networks where membership is 'explicit', i.e., accompanied by conscious decisions and reflections. Networks may also be considered to be 'transparent' or 'opaque'. A transparent network is one where the identity of members is known or readily ascertained. An opaque network is one where a member or the external observer does not know nor have the means to know, the identities of the members. There may also be cases where one or more members have access to information about members' identities and other members do not or do so only partially. Concerning (v), it may be the case that individual social actors are members of several social networks. It may be the case that there are formal relations connecting networks. I leave it to the reader to reflect upon these possibilities and to come up with examples.

5 *What Is the Distinction between a 'Social Network' and a 'Social System'?*

The term social network and social system are commonly used in the social sciences, often with the implicit assumption that they are different theoretical entities. The use of the term 'social system' implies that, in some sense, one is referring to an autonomous whole. Concerning social networks, it is important to ask who is distinguishing the network in question. Is it the external observer or is it some or all of the members? In social systems, such as clubs and societies or corporate institutions, the participants are capable of consciously acknowledging their membership. The systems are organisationally closed and reproduce themselves as stable unities. If an observer-defined social network is an organisationally closed system, the network is a social system, otherwise, it is not. In other words, whereas all social systems can be modelled as social networks, not all social networks are social systems. This concept can be recursively applied, i.e., just as there may be networks of networks, there may be social networks of social networks (collectives of collectives).

6 *A Brief Critique of 'Connectivism' and 'Actor-Network Theory'*

In the context of a discussion of social networks, it is relevant to mention 'connectivism' and 'actor-network theory'. Both are concerned with human behaviour and both use the term 'network'. However, neither of them is concerned with social networks as defined here. Both have in common the feature that nodes can be any 'thing' and arcs can represent any relationship between nodes that can be considered as a connection or link.

'Connectivism' (or 'connectivity theory') is a loosely formulated theory of learning that asserts that, in the age of the internet and related technologies, learning is a process of "connecting specialized nodes or information sources" (Georges Siemens, 2005). The theory, unlike many other theories of learning, does not refer to particular brain activity or cognitive processes. It does emphasise that in a web-based environment, learning may employ strategies that are 'nonlinear' but there is no reference to the existing literature on learning strategies. The concept of 'nonlinear learning' can be traced back to the seminal work of Pask and Scott (1972) on 'holist' and 'serialist' learning strategies.

The creator of Actor-Network Theory (ATN), Bruno Latour, has declared that ATN is not about actors or networks, and is not a theory (Latour, 2005). Rather, it is a tool for describing social action in a particular context, such as a laboratory or other work place.

7 *Concluding Comments: The 'Global Conversation'*

The concept of a global conversation refers to something that is emerging but is still at a stage of immaturity. As a social network, it is fragmented: technologically (because not all can participate),[91] culturally (participants are separated by language and by self-ascribed cultural identities), and ideologically. Sadly, in our world, there are pathological belief systems that engender conflict, rather than harmony (Scott, 2015). If our world is to survive and thrive, we need social networks that afford conversations that educate, that enlighten. I say more about the challenges we face in the next part.

Part 10 Some Sociocybernetic Understanding of Possible World Futures

1 *Introduction*

In this part, I set out some ideas about how sociocybernetics can contribute to understanding possible world futures, ideas first developed in Scott (2009b). A central concept in cybernetics is 'governance', the art of steersmanship. As conceived by Ashby, Beer and others, this art is concerned with the management of variety. How do we face the challenge of managing all the variety that makes up 'possible world futures'? The distinction between first order and second order cybernetics makes clear that there are two levels to this challenge: (i) the variety and complexity of first order, observed systems (ii) the variety and complexity of second order systems, the interactions within and between human observers.

Already, the distinction between the two levels has reduced variety. Attempting to understand possible world futures with first order studies only, omits the challenges of bringing about change through social action. Using second order studies to address the challenges of bringing about social change can only be fruitful insofar as relevant models and data are available from first order studies. I begin by considering what it means to be holistic about global problems. I then briefly overview what first order models and data are telling us, and what some second order models and data are telling us. The part goes

91 Some 59% of the world's population use the internet. For data by region, see https://www.visualcapitalist.com/the-next-billion-internet-users-worldwide/ (accessed 17/08/20).

on to outline ways in which sociocybernetics can address the problems thus summarised.

2 *Being Holistic about Global Problems*

One of the founding predications of the cybernetics and systems movement is that systemic problems need to be addressed holistically (Beer, 1967; Mulej and Kajzer 1998; Scott, 2002b).

Concerning the need to be both holistic and global, Luhmann (1989) very clearly warns of two dangers: (i) failure to 'resonate' with the ecosystem (not being global enough in our concerns); (ii) too much resonance between social systems (not being holistic enough to dampen unfruitful noise and 'excitement'). Examples of (i) are many: being parochial concerning one's own ecological niche; focussing on one issue (e.g., 'global warming' or 'poverty') but not taking cognisance of related issues (e.g., 'educational opportunities' or 'political freedoms'). Examples of (ii) are also many: the promotion of one scientific discipline over another, the promotion of one political ideology over another, in general, the tendency to work in self-promoting silos.

'Being holistic' lacks meaning if the theoretical ideal lacks a praxis. The problem is that no observer can step outside and observe the whole of which she is a part. However, she can *intend* to be holistic. Actualising holism requires a cognitive/affective centre around which the many facets and levels of our concerns may cohere as insight, intuition and commitment. I believe that the perceived need for a holistic centring can itself serve as such a centre. For practitioners it is sufficient to intend to be holistic – and to share that intent – in order to make fruitful cooperation possible. It is no accident that the word 'holism', has the same etymological root as the word 'holy' (Old English, *halig*, whole, hale, healthy).

Sociocybernetics offers guiding principles that bear on the question of how a community of observers can establish and maintain consensus, including:

1. Ashby's Law of Requisite Variety: only variety can destroy (control) variety.
2. Scott's Laws of Observation and Action:
   - There is always a bigger picture.
   - There is always another level of detail.
   - There is always another perspective.
   - There is always error.
   - There is always the unexpected.
3. von Foerster's ethical imperative: act so as to increase the choices.
4. von Foerster's corollary to his ethical imperative: in a community, A is better off when B is better off.

3 *First Order Problems*

Modern economies are based on forms of capitalism where returns on investment lead to reinvestment with the goal of continued economic growth. To keep it going, this growth requires a source of labour, much of it skilled and professional, together with the reinvestment of profits and readily available sources of energy and raw materials. With this growth, the rich get richer and continue to do so.[92]

Many developing countries suffer from economic exploitation by developed countries and corrupt government. Both developed and developing nations are investing in education and training and are creating relatively wealthy middle classes as well as super-rich plutocracies. There is a flow of labour, as legal and illegal immigrants from Africa, Eastern Europe and Asia enter Western Europe. There are flows from South America into North America. There are flows into Australia.

The switch from hunter-gatherer societies, over millennia, together with a growth in world population, has made humankind net consumers of the earth's resources. That is, in the long term, economic growth as currently pursued is not sustainable. Forests are cut down, species are lost, oceans are depleted of fish stocks, fertile lands become deserts. In recent times, fossil fuels, as a source of stored energy and desirable by-products such as fertilisers, plastic and pharmaceuticals, have fed economic growth and continue to do so. The use of such fuels and other resources has triggered climate change, widespread pollution and damage to the ozone layer. The problems associated with continued economic growth are exacerbated by continued population growth. It has been estimated by some that, if everyone was enjoying the same standard of living as now enjoyed by 'developed' parts of the world, it would take five Earths to support the current population.[93]

In March 2008, a conference on the topic *From Global Warming to Global Policy* was convened by the World Political Forum and the Club of Rome and chaired by President Mikhail Gorbachev in Turin on March 28–29 2008. I quote from the final statement.

"The participants concluded that the world has entered a period in which the dramatic scale, complexity and speed of change caused by human activities threaten the fragile environmental and ecological systems of the planet on which we depend. It is urgent therefore that the world community should agree rapidly on strategies and effective action to avert irreversible change in

92 For detailed discussions of the harm this does to society at large, see Stiglitz (2013), Piketty (2015) and Dorling (2015).

93 This estimate dates from 2008.

world systems, brought about by accelerating climate change, the ecosystems crisis, the depletion of energy resources and the diminishing availability of water, the degradation of environments across the world, persistent poverty and deprivation and the rising gulf between rich and poor within and between countries. Also, global population is in the midst of a transition from explosive growth to a new paradigm of development, never before experienced by humankind."[94]

Since then, there have been many more such warnings as the work of activists has raised awareness of the issues within the general public. Figure 16 is intended to be a simple holistic overview of what some current first order models and data are telling us about possible world futures.

4 *Second Order Problems*

Second order problems concern human behaviour and social interactions where the participants are observing systems with beliefs and who follow institutionalised behaviour patterns in the pursuit of goals, some of which may be consciously articulated, some of which are the non-conscious consequences of participation in a culture and genetic heritage. In some communities, participants are encouraged to learn and be creative, in others less so.

Some important second order issues are:

1. differing kinds and levels of social and cultural development, including differences in quality of life, access to health services and education, problems of identity and social conflict, for example, as set out in the hypothesis of there being a 'clash of civilisations' (Huntington, 1997).
2. pathological belief systems that institutionalise ignorance, prejudice, discrimination, and conflict.[95]
3. as noted by Luhmann, the problem of 'noise' and redundancy in the 'marketplace' of ideas.
4. the problem of empowerment for social action, as in the lack of democratic forms of government and lack of access to opportunities for personal development.

These problems can be summed up in terms of two cybernetic principles: evil is that which restricts the right of actors to interact (Pask, 1991, p. 1) and "Act always so as to increase the number of choices" (von Foerster, 2003, p. 227).

94 In 2018, the Club of Rome published *The Climate Emergency Plan*, https://clubofrome.org/publication/the-climate-emergency-plan/ (accessed 24/11/2020).

95 In Scott (2015), I use concepts from sociocybernetics to analyse what I see as pathological about the Abrahamic faiths.

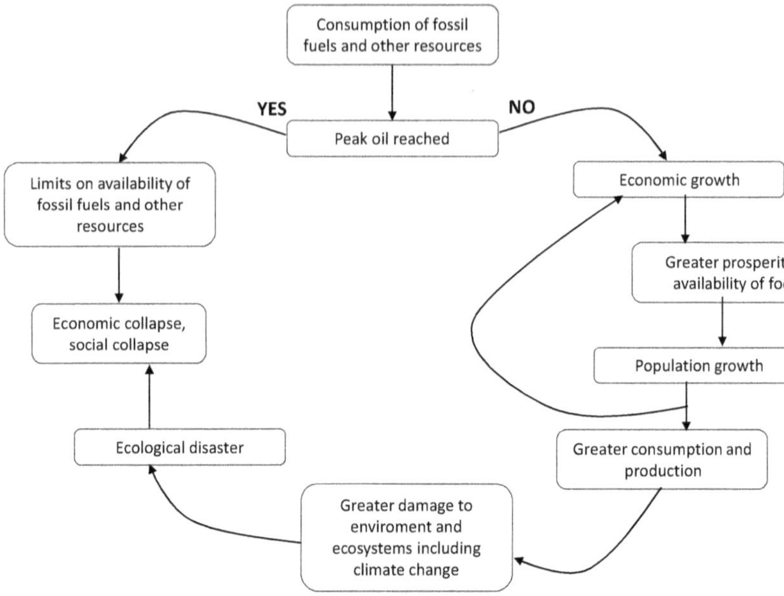

FIGURE 16 An attempt at a simple holistic overview of some global problems

The two principles are complementary. Both are predicated on two key assumptions: (i) there is a shared gene pool (ii) people (social actors) are, at least in part, socially constructed. The first principle helps to identify blocks and constraints. The second principle helps to guide creative, positive action. Both are, in essence, corollaries of Ashby's (1956) Law of Requisite Variety, "Only variety can control variety." Variety is controlled by identifying redundancies, patterns, and lawfulness. Hence the importance of education (Latin, *educare*, to lead out) and the importance of concepts from cybernetics that provide transdisciplinary and metadisciplinary clarity and coherence to manage the variety of theories and models in the academic market place.[96]

How humans form and maintain systems of belief is a complex business, with rational and non-rational aspects (Wolpert, 2006). Even belief systems that are rationally constructed may, in the longer term, turn out to be flawed and misguided. A case in point is the faith of economists in classic economic models based on the concept of equilibrium between supply and demand.

96 In Scott (2014), mentioned in part 2, I set out some of the concepts from cybernetics which I believe should be part of the spiral curriculum that, ideally, is revisited throughout an individual's education from primary to higher levels, at each stage with greater sophistication and detail.

Ormerod (2005) points out that failure to predict the future is endemic in the business world. As stated in Scott's fourth law (above), "There is always the unexpected". The world, as a whole, continues to surprise us.

5 *Looking for Solutions*

What might be done?[97] As economies collapse, nation states and coalitions thereof may well go on a war footing where new orders of doing things are imposed, for example, rationing of food and energy, bans on travel, investment in alternative forms of energy supply, and imposition of birth control. As noted above, hopefully, there may also be an accelerated process of education, awareness-raising and political empowerment that includes the recognition that some belief systems such as 'individualism' are unacceptable. ('Individualism' is the social disease, currently legitimised and encouraged in all parts of the world, of seeking, as an individual or member of a family, to become rich and powerful relative to one's neighbours.) Legislative and economic reforms of some kind will be required. There is also the requirement to educate, raise awareness, and change belief systems.

The tough question is, "How do we (humankind) change our practices while the world is falling apart?" The battle for 'correct thinking' has to be won as only 'correct thinking' in the long term leads to 'correct action'. The populace in the developed countries with access to resources such as mass education and mass communication systems are not stupid or necessarily ignorant. They are seduced and manipulated by consumerism and the lifestyles portrayed in popular entertainment and advertising. Insofar as there is a growing awareness that disasters of one kind or another are imminent, this is accompanied by feelings of alienation and disempowerment. We will need a rapid change in popular consciousness delivering the right messages as disasters strike such that politicians and corporate leaders are obliged to change their ways.

It is of value for all of us, as 'ordinary people' to engage in discussion about these issues. There are underlying empirical and logical truths as sketched out above, that need to be understood and promulgated. The 'right thinking' produced by education will lead to the 'right action', including the action of promoting the right thinking and of commanding the means to do so. This requires educational activities to go hand in hand with the evolution of more effective means for democratic participation. The populous, made aware of what is required, must find its voice. We need positive feedback cycles, where the demand for better education and more informed knowledge about what

---

97 As I write this in June, 2020, the world is facing the challenges of the covid-19 pandemic, which is adding another dimension to the world's existing challenges.

is happening and why leads to demands for even better education and better knowledge sharing about ways of translating right thinking into right action.

Concerning 'right thinking', I have identified two fallacies which I believe need to addressed and corrected:

1. The fallacy of the particular: "I am all right because the problems are happening somewhere else."
2. The fallacy of the general: "Humankind will survive somehow."

In relative terms, Fallacy 1 was perhaps once true but is false now that, globally, as noted below, "Everything is connected to everything else." Concerning Fallacy 2, it is possibly true but, as a pious hope, it can blind us to an awareness of the great cost in human lives and suffering that will be (and is being) paid as part of the survival of the species.

There follows a brief listing of some aspects of possible solutions that I have come across in the literature and in the media. There is not space here to present them in any detail. I present them as a means of promoting further discussion.

1. Switching to renewable forms of energy.
2. Using alternative forms of production and waste disposal that are truly sustainable, possibly using nanotechnologies and 'synthetic biology'.
3. Using just and humane forms of birth control to reduce the global population.
4. Only interacting with the ecosystem in ways that are sustainable and healing of damage already inflicted.
5. Education for social justice and quality of life, rather than for the individualism of wealth accumulation and consumerism.
6. Education and legislation for empowerment as part of more effective forms of democratic government
7. A move away from the economic growth emphasis of modern capitalism as embodied in 'limited companies', 'corporations' and 'shareholders' towards cooperative forms of institution.
8. New forms of tithing or taxation that change damaging behaviours and/or release resources that can be invested in developing sustainable ways of doing things.[98]

6 *Concluding Comments*

Given the scale of the problems at both first and second order levels, mankind is facing major disasters on a global scale. Amelioration of these disasters will, in the limit, be in the hands of whatever communities emerge and survive locally. More global solutions are thinkable. However, as these entail a radical

98 See, for example, the recommendations made by Joseph Stiglitz (2013).

re-appraisal and re-education about what it is to be human, it is not obvious at this stage that these global solutions are doable. It may be too late for such a global transformation of human consciousness to be achieved. It may be that, as proposed by Morrison (1999) and many others, there are intrinsic limitations on the extent to which the human species can embody the beliefs needed to ensure its survival.

A majority of commentators appear to see no alternative to capitalism, economic competition, continually striving for more, for better 'standards of living'.[99] Some do question the values and their relative importance. What is more important; a high income or safety from harm, riches or job satisfaction? And so on. There are alternatives to secular, materialistic capitalist ways of life. For example, there are those based on the concept of sustainable living, abiding by Commoner's (1971) Four Laws of Ecology. I cite them here as key holistic, systemic, cybernetic ideas that are essential for understanding how we might manage the variety in global systems. Ideas such as these should be vital parts of educational curricula, from the cradle to the grave:

1. "Everything is connected to everything else." There is one biosphere for all living organisms and what affects one, affects all.
2. "Everything must go somewhere." There is no 'waste' in nature and there is no 'away' to which things can be thrown.
3. "Nature knows best." Humankind has fashioned technologies to improve upon nature, but the changes are proving to be detrimental to that system.
4. "There is no such thing as a free lunch". In nature, both sides of the equation must balance; for every gain there is a cost and all debts are eventually paid.[100]

Part 11 Sociocybernetic Understandings of Culture

> Warfare is an utterly stupid method of settling differences of interest between different nations.
>
> GEORGE H. MEAD

•••

99 The final communiqué of the G7 Conference, Japan, 2016, set 'global growth as a priority for dealing with threats to the world's economy and security'.

100 For more about the life and work of Barry Commoner, see the article in Wikipedia. http://en.wikipedia.org/wiki/Barry_Commoner. Accessed August 29th, 2016.

> Accumulation of wealth at one pole is at the same time accumulation of misery, agony of toil, slavery, ignorance, brutality, mental degradation, at the opposite pole.
>
> KARL MARX

∴

1 *Introduction*

As I write, individuals and collectives around the planet are oppressing, physically violating and killing other humans. At the same time, as outlined in part 10, our very home, our ecosystem, is under threat, from pollution, from climate change, from pandemics and the unsustainable consumption of resources. Meanwhile, the global economic system carries on largely with business as usual; the gap between rich and poor increases, while some 98% of all financial transactions are speculations (bets).[101] In this part, I wish to use sociocybernetic concepts to address issues concerning cultural transmissions and transformations. By 'culture' I mean the habits and values, often tacit, of a particular collective or community as expressed in individual behaviours, interactions and the use and production of 'artefacts' in the broadest sense (for example, encompassing spoken and written texts and other symbolic forms, and found or constructed concrete objects). I believe that to bring about any profound or lasting change in how humans treat each other and the planet that is their home, a culture of mutual respect and cooperation needs to be engendered and nurtured, while pathological cultural manifestations need to be identified and eradicated. In section 2, I consider conceptions and definitions of *culture*, *society* and *social system*. In section 3, I consider the relations between culture and 'personality'. In section 4, I proffer some sociocybernetic understandings of culture and social systems. In section 5, I discuss cultural transmissions and transformations, considering what factors lead some cultures to persist, while others are subject to changes, some of which are gradual, some of which are rapid and disruptive. This leads me to a discussion of interactions between cultures, including what some authorities refer to as 'the clash of civilisations' (Huntington, 1997) and 'cultural imperialism' (Tomlinson, 2012).

In section 6, I argue for the need for effective 'intercultural conversations', where there is a genuine openness to learning about other cultures, and to

101 Lietear, Arnsberger et al (2012).

the criticism and modification of pathological practices. I use concepts from cybernetics to characterise what I mean by 'pathological'.

2 *Conceptions and Definitions of 'Culture'*

An examination of the literature shows that formulating satisfactory conceptions and definitions of culture is complicated and contentious. For example, it is usual to attempt to distinguish the biological from the cultural, where the biological refers to that which is genetically inherited and cultural to that which is learned from interaction between an organism and its social environment. I say 'organism', because many species have a discernible culture in this sense. Here, my focus is on the human animal, much of whose culture is conserved and communicated symbolically, using a variety of media. Much is also communicated through behavioural and affective interaction, often tacitly, without explicit awareness. This can be seen to begin in the ways parents nurture their infants by creating comforting, secure environments, with established routines for providing care (Newsom and Newsom, 1979). The combination of symbolic, behavioural and affective influences (Humberto Maturana refers to 'languaging' and 'emotioning' in this context)[102] continues to communicate and reinforce cultural practices throughout a human's life.

I proposed my definition in the Introduction. This was to provide some initial orientation for the discussion. Here is a selection of some other definitions that I found after an internet search.[103]

> Culture may be defined as the totality of the mental and physical reactions and activities that characterize the behavior of individuals composing a social group collectively and individually in relations to their natural environment, to other groups, to members of the group itself and of each individual to himself. It also includes the products of these activities and their role in the life of the groups.
>
> FRANZ BOAZ

> Culture or civilization, taken in its wide ethnographic sense is that complex whole which includes knowledge, belief, art, morals, law, custom, and any other capabilities and habits acquired by man as a member of society.
>
> E. B. TYLER

102 See Maturana and Verden-Zoller (2008).

103 More recently, my friend, Bernd Hornung referred me to Kroeber and Kluckhohn's (1952) book which provides a critical review of concepts and definitions of 'culture'. I have not yet had chance to examine it in detail.

> Culture denotes an historically transmitted pattern of meanings embodied in symbols, a system of inherited conceptions expressed in symbolic forms by means of which men communicate, perpetuate, and develop their knowledge about and attitudes toward life.
>
> CLIFFORD GEERTZ

> Sociology understands culture as the languages, customs, beliefs, rules, arts, knowledge, and collective identities and memories developed by members of all social groups that make their social environments meaningful.
>
> AMERICAN SOCIOLOGICAL ASSOCIATION, http://www.asanet.org/topics/culture

Some of the definitions are quite narrow. Only the definition by Franz Boas is as comprehensive as the one I propose. It is also worth noting that these definitions overlap with how other writers define 'society' and 'social system'. Here are some examples.

> Society is a concept used to describe the structured relations and institutions among a large community of people which cannot be reduced to a simple collection or aggregation of individuals.
>
> GIDDENS AND SUTTON (2017) Essential Concepts in Sociology https://revisesociology.com/2017/07/07/what-is-society-sociology/ ...

> A society is a large group of people who live together in an organized way, making decisions about how to do things and sharing the work that needs to be done.
>
> https://dictionary.cambridge.org/dictionary/english/society

> A social system is the patterned series of interrelationships existing between individuals, groups, and institutions and forming a coherent whole.
>
> https://www.merriam-webster.com/dictionary/social%20system

Talcott Parsons is relevant to my discussion because he explicitly wished to develop a theory of social systems that draws on general systems theory and cybernetics, as stated here:

> The fundamental starting point is the concept of social systems of action. The interaction of individual actors, that is, takes place under such conditions that it is possible to treat such a process of interaction as a system in

> the scientific sense and subject it to the same order of theoretical analysis which has been successfully applied to other types of systems in other sciences.
>
> TALCOTT PARSONS (1951, p. 1)

It remains a moot point as to whether or not his starting point is justifiable and to what extent he was successful in his aims. Parsons does, however, take pains to define his key concepts. His understanding of culture vis-à-vis a social system is stated in the following:

> A social system consists in a plurality of individual actors interacting with each other in a situation which has at least a physical or environmental aspect, actors who are motivated in terms of a tendency to the "optimization of gratification" and whose relation to their situations, including each other, is defined and mediated in terms of a system of culturally structured and shared symbols. Thus conceived, a social system is only one of three aspects of the structuring of a completely concrete system of social action. The other two are the personality systems of the individual actors and the cultural system which is built into their action. Each of the three must be considered to be an independent focus of the organization of the elements of the action system in the sense that no one of them is theoretically reducible to terms of one or a combination of the other two. Each is indispensable to the other two in the sense that without personalities and culture there would be no social system and so on around the roster of logical possibilities.
>
> op. cit., p. 3

Parsons's formulation has the merit of wishing to distinguish social systems, culture, and personality systems and show their relations. I, myself, find his concept of motivation as the tendency to the 'optimisation of gratification' limited and unsatisfactory, based as it is on Freudian psychoanalytic theories.

Niklas Luhmann, in his theory of social systems (which very much takes as its starting point the ideas of Talcott Parsons), whilst acknowledging the difficulties of trying to define 'culture', does find a place for the concept, as follows:

> An intervening requirement mediates between language and interaction – a supply of possible themes that is available for quick and readily understandable reception in concrete processes. We would like to call the supplied themes *culture*, and, it is reserved specifically for the purposes of communication, semantics. Thus, an earnest, considerable semantics

> is a part of culture, namely, of what is handed down to us by the history of concepts and ideas.
>
> LUHMANN (1995) p. 163[104]

> The communication that is incessantly stimulated forms islands of comprehensibility in a sea of meaningfully indicated possibilities, and these islands, as culture in the broadest sense, facilitate the initiation and ending of interaction. Cultural forms, later above all the communication media of writing and printing, ceased to be fixed specifically to interaction and thus enable interaction and precisely thereby enable meaning specific differentiation within society.
>
> op. cit ., pp. 417–418

This appears to me to be a somewhat narrow conception of culture. It minimises the role of oral storytelling in preliterate cultures. It also fails to acknowledge the 'culture' that is shared and transmitted tacitly and nonverbally, for example, in how complex knowledge and skills, such as hunting and culinary practices, are passed on.[105]

Having seen variety and overlap in the conceptions of culture, society and social system, we can at least allow that they all share a concern with social life and the meanings that humans find therein. The culture/social system may evolve to create social institutions that serve different functions and empower or impose constraints on what social actors may say and do. However, it is the culture that determines how law-abiding the members are, to what extent they acknowledge and agree with any freedoms that are granted or constraints that are imposed.

Parsons and Luhmann employ the macro-sociological concept of the differentiation of society into 'functional subsystems', each with a different 'code', or binary value system. For example, Luhmann distinguishes, amongst others, the science subsystem (with code, true/false), the economics subsystem (code, pay/not pay), and the legal system (code, legal/illegal). As mentioned in parts 1 and 6, detailed discussion of these macro-sociological theories is beyond the scope of this publication, for two reasons (i) they are complex and controversial, and (ii) I prefer the Paskian idea of embodied psychosocial unities,

---

104 For a detailed discussion of how Luhmann's concept of culture can be understood from his several passing references, see Laermans (2007).

105 For a discussion of these processes in a modern, organisational setting, see Cook and Yanow (2011). There is a wider literature, known as "cultural-historical activity theory", that is relevant here. It has origins in the work of Lev Vygotsky. See https://en.wikipedia.org/wiki/Cultural-historical_activity_theory (accessed 28/05/2018).

differentiated by the conversational domains that define them, rather than the concept of an impersonal autonomous functional subsystem.[106]

In recent years, the 'institutional logics perspective' has developed, which stands as an alternative to the macro-sociology of Parsons and Luhmann, and is akin to Pask's approach. An institutional logic is "the socially constructed, historical patterns of cultural symbols and material practices, including assumptions, values, and beliefs by which individuals and organizations provide meaning to their daily activity, organize time and space, and reproduce their lives and experiences," (Thornton, Ocasio et al, 2012, p. 2). The authors develop "a recursive theory of society that incorporates individuals and organizations" (op. cit., p. 50).

A seminal work in this approach was the introduction of the concept of "an institutional grammar", based on the view that "institutions are enduring regularities of human action and situation structured by rules, norms, and shared strategies, as well as by the physical world" (Crawford and Ostrom. 1995). The authors propose a syntax (a set of rules) for this grammar, where each rule has five components: 'attributes' (those to whom the rule applies), 'deontic' (type of rule: must, may or must not), 'aims' (the particular actions to which the deontic applies), 'conditions' (the variables which define when, where, how, and to what extent an action is permitted, obligatory, or forbidden), and 'or else' (the variables which define the sanctions to be imposed for not following a rule).[107]

All shared strategies can be written as attributes, aim, conditions; all norms can be written as attributes, deontic, aim, conditions; all rules can be written as deontic, aim, conditions, or else. Note the accumulation: norms contain the attributes of strategies, rules contain the attributes of norms (op. cit. pp. 583–584). I trust the reader recognises the general cybernetic form of these syntactic rules (see the description of a TOTE unit in part 4).

A given social system, such as a nation state, may have a culture that is more or less homogeneous (a monoculture) or heterogenous (a multi-culture). Although some similarities of attitude and behaviour are required for the concept of culture to be applicable at all, there are a variety of ways in which one can find differences, for example, related to gender, age, socio-economic

106 Pask's commentaries about social systems are dispersed and relatively few, given that his primary interest was in the interactions of social actors. For a discussion of the conversations that constitute different domains of activity within society (science, art, religion and so on), see Pask (1979b). For a detailed discussion of conversational domains and the relations between them, see Pask (1976).

107 There is also a body of work on the 'dynamics of norms', their formation, maintenance, metamorphosis, and dissolution, which uses game theory, decision theory and computer modelling. See, e.g., Bicchieri, Jeffrey et al, eds. (1997).

status, faith or lack of it, family and kinship relations, occupation and interests. Culture can be conceived of, then, as the set of concepts that is passed on from generation to generation, including concepts whose role is to construct and reconstruct other concepts such that the whole body of concepts (knowledge and skills, beliefs and practices) is itself self-reproducing. At each scale of thinking, from individual to collectives, the psychosocial unity can be analysed for its ways of working as a social/cultural system. Its embodiment in a set of biomechanical unities can be analysed for its ways of working as an organisationally closed system that sustains the psychosocial unity. As Norbert Wiener (1950) eloquently expresses it, "Our tissues change as we live: the food we eat and the air we breathe become flesh of our flesh and bone of our bone, and the momentary elements of our flesh and bone pass out of our body every day with our excreta. We are but whirlpools in a river of ever-flowing water. We are not stuff that abides, but patterns that perpetuate themselves." Both psychosocial unities and biomechanical unities are patterns that perpetuate themselves. In societies, these patterns are perpetuated collectively using all manner of biomechanical extensions guided by psychosocial activity: agricultural production, mechanical production, sewage disposal systems, defence systems and so on.

With this concept of what is a society, we have neatly voided the distinction between cultures and social systems. I see this as an elegant and satisfying way of avoiding the conceptual difficulties involved in trying to define them separately. However, I do not doubt that social theorists will continue to use the two terms for different kinds of emphasis.

It would be remiss of me at this point if I failed to mention other approaches to social systems/culture/society, which are explicitly based on systems thinking and cybernetics. Seminal work applying systems theoretic concepts in sociology was carried out by Walter Buckley (1967). The general idea of the value of a sociocybernetic approach has been promulgated by Felix Geyer (1995) and, more recently by Bernd Hornung (2019). I do not have space here to provide commentary but encourage the reader to find out more.

As noted in part 1, there is a large and varied field of systems thinking, some of which explicitly draws on cybernetics. Much of this work is concerned with the understanding of organisations and social institutions but, although it has evident overlaps with organisational psychology and cultural anthropology, it tends to exist as a discourse separate from the discipline of sociology. For a very useful guide to this field, see Ramage and Shipp (2009).[108]

108 The authors include several cyberneticians in the compendium, including Stafford Beer, but, interestingly, fail to include Pask. I suspect summarising his work and ideas proved

Stafford Beer, known as 'the father of management cybernetics' developed a generic model of a viable system (the Viable System Model or VSM) that can be applied recursively from the level of an individual up to the level of a nation state. The model is based on the workings of the human nervous system and how, in real time, it uses 'the management of variety' to monitor its internal environment and its interactions with its external environment, whilst maintaining itself as a viable organisation (Beer, 1972). Beer's work continues to be developed and applied, and it is recognised as being particularly relevant in the context of the challenges faced by humankind today.[109]

3 *Culture and Personality*

Developmental psychologists and paediatricians classify infants as having different, largely biologically given, 'temperaments'.[110] As the infant matures to adulthood, under the impact of the culture or cultures in which she lives, and other life experiences, the temperament evolves into a 'personality', a form of personhood, a 'self' with a particular identity. Here, following the ideas of Peirce, G. H. Mead, von Foerster, Pask, and others, the self is considered to be a form of dynamic organisation capable of signifying itself and others as selves, that is, taking itself as an object for observation and contemplation, and others as potential partners in the shared expectations required for social interaction.

As discussed in earlier parts, Pask makes a useful analytic distinction between a 'psychological individual' (P-Individual or psychosocial unity) the 'mechanical individual' (M-Individual or biomechanical unity) that embodies it. The system of concepts, that is the self, include concepts of the self.[111] It is the embodiment of a self that is the source of feelings and emotions. To emphasise that the P/M distinction is analytic, made for theoretical convenience, Pask would often say, "A thought is a feeling".[112]

---

too much of a challenge.

109 For a very user-friendly introduction to Beer's life and work, see Beer and Leonard (2019).

110 Following pioneering work by Thomas, Chess and Birch (1968), there has been a wealth of research and theorising about infant temperaments and developmental outcomes. See, for example, Rothbart (2012).

111 I like this aphorism from Peirce, "Accordingly, just as we say that a body is in motion, and not that motion is in a body, we ought to say that we are in thought, and not that thoughts are in us," Hoopes, op. cit. p. 71.

112 There is a considerable literature about feelings and emotions, with roots in the ideas of Charles Darwin. For an understanding of the physiology at the molecular level, I recommend Pert (1999). For competing views about how to classify emotions and the extent to which emotions are socially constructed, see Ekman (2004) and Barrett (2018). For recent work in neuroscience that shows that 'emotion' and 'cognition' are not functionally

The particular structure and content of an embodied self at any moment gives her a particular personality or identity. Concerning the evolving dynamics of the self, von Foerster notes, "At every moment, I can choose who I am" (Poerksen, 2003), George Gurdjieff and others (see, for example, Ouspensky, 1947) note that the self is a multiplicity, a collective of perspectives, which has to be managed to provide personal integrity around a set of values. Individuals vary in the extent to which they are capable of such self-observation and self-management. Cultures vary in the extent to which such reflexive work on the self is encouraged or acknowledged as common practice (for example, in meditation). Concerning the structure of a self and the dynamics of self-awareness (consciousness), von Foerster (2003, p. 257) states that "'I' is the relation between self and observation of self" (or, using the terminology of G. H. Mead, 'I' is the process that computes/describes 'me' as a product).

As discussed in part 8, conceptualisation is an ongoing dynamic, heterarchical system, an inner conversation in which concepts are constructed and reconstructed (remembered) and applied, with much of this activity going on in a non-conscious manner. The concepts that are in awareness are those about which there is some uncertainty. When the inner conversation reaches agreement, temporary hierarchies of concepts are formed, with goals and subgoals, that guide directed thought and action. One has decided to do something. The accompanying process in the brain/body system is that previously heterarchical, asynchronous processes have become synchronised. In outer conversations, as coordination, cooperation and conflict occur, two or more social actors become temporarily synchronised with each other; they 'language' together (Maturana), they 'provoke each other' (Pask),[113] they engage in 'language games' (Wittgenstein), they engage in the 'dance' of social interaction (von Foerster). They constitute a collective. Recurring forms of interaction lead to the establishment of a shared culture with social institutions, and the norms (rules) that constitute them. This sharing of cultural expectations can be found between two persons, as in a marriage, in small groups, such as families, clubs and friendship groups, as well as in large collectives, business organisations, and whole societies. Wittgenstein (1953) tells us that languages are 'forms of life', collections of 'language games', the shared ways

---

distinct, see Pessoa (2013). Durbridge (1994) proposes the term 'confect' to capture the idea that concepts (cognitive processes) always have an affective component.

113 In Pask's conversation theory, an understanding within or between P-Individuals corresponds to the synchronisation of processes within or between M-Individuals. Understandings are examples of 'information transfer' (see Pask, 1975b, p. 78). In later writings, Pask describes P-Individuals as being organisationally closed but 'informationally open', in that they can indeed share understandings of each other's concepts.

in which humans communicate and cooperate. Languages are too complex to be fully captured in grammars or dictionaries. Wittgenstein's conclusions about the human condition are remarkably similar to those of the cultural anthropologist, Edward T. Hall (1959), who pioneered the study of non-verbal communication within and between cultures. Hall tells us that people from different cultures inhabit different 'sensory worlds', making it imperative that we develop deep understandings of those worlds. "Communication occurs simultaneously on different levels of consciousness, ranging from full awareness to out-of-awareness (and uses) a series of delicately controlled, culturally conditioned servomechanisms that keeps life on an even keel, much like the automatic pilot on an aeroplane" (Hall, 1969, p. 5).

A particular virtue of Pask's, 'bottom-up' understanding of social systems as conversations, in contrast to the 'top down' macrosociologies of Parsons, Luhmann, and others, is that, in any particular situation, one or more social actors can be identified as being responsible, as leaders, for the system's behaviour. For this to be the case, we must thoroughly understand how the system behaves and who is maintaining that behaviour. If we are indeed autonomous selves, we should not just accept the status of being victims of 'the system'; we can work to change it. All who are involved in a social system's working have some responsibility for its effects: the oppressors and the oppressed; the rich and the poor; the educated and the ignorant; the wise and the foolish. "Any situation in which 'A' objectively exploits 'B' or hinders his and her pursuit of self-affirmation as a responsible person is one of oppression" (Freire, 1996, p. 37). "The structure of domination (false consciousness) is maintained by its own mechanical unconscious functionality," Freire (ibid, p. 33). "The energy of the oppressed is an instrument for their critical discovery that both they and their oppressors are manifestations of dehumanisation" (Freire, ibid, p. 30).

4 *Cultural Transmissions and Transformations*

> The world is a symbolic world in the sense that it consists of conceptually organised, rule-bound belief systems about what exists, about how to get to goals, about what is to be valued. There is no way, none, in which a human being could possibly master that world without the aid and assistance of others for, in fact, that world is others.
>
> JEROME BRUNER (1985, p. 32)

∴

As argued above, cultures (qua social systems or societies) are self-perpetuating. Their structure may vary as they adapt to changing circumstances but their organisational closure is conserved. They reproduce themselves, more or less successfully. The biomechanical fabric decays and dies and is replaced. The beliefs and behaviours of the culture are passed on from generation to generation. The newborn are nurtured and socialised. The subsystems that support these processes vary in detail from culture to culture. They include the family, the education system, and the processes of induction and training that accompany being a member of a particular organisation and occupying a particular social role. None of the systems and processes is perfect. Examples of successful cultural transmissions are many, for example, the traditions of the great faiths and associated civilisations (Huntington, 1997), and the long-term stability, over centuries, of some preliterate societies (see, for example, Rappaport, 1967).

Although many cultures are long-lived, they are still subject to change. Some cultures suffer more drastic changes, to the point that the culture itself may cease to exist. With conquest, the old culture may go underground or become 'syncretised' (amalgamated) with the new. The new ruling elite may adopt the old culture as their own. The old culture may be forgotten. However, aspects of a culture can be coded and preserved in books and other texts. The texts may then be discovered at a later date and the culture re-embodied. For example, many Christians have become converts from reading the Bible, not from interacting with other Christians. The importation of Greek and Roman texts helped transform European culture in the period known as the Renaissance (14th–17th centuries).

Transformations occur for a variety of reasons: conflicts and schisms over forms of belief, wars over territory or succession, colonisation, revolutions, the impact of education and innovations, ecological disasters, epidemics, migration, population displacement and replacement, changing demographics, secularisation, fashion, peer pressure, persecution, enslavement, ethnic cleansing and genocide, globalisation.[114] In some cases, the beliefs and practices of a culture lead to its demise. The Shakers, a Christian Sect created in 1747, practised celibacy. In 1961, the last Shaker community stopped accepting new members. In 2017, it was reported that there were only two Shakers still alive.[115] Cultures can also collapse because their beliefs and practices are inherently negative and life denying. Examples can be found in the rise and fall of fascism in European countries in the 20th century. "Evil is not destructive to

114 For more on this theme, see Berger and Huntington (eds.) (2002).

115 See https://www.smithsonianmag.com/smart-news/there-are-only-two-shakers-left-world-180961701/ (accessed 15/05/2020).

the good alone but inevitably destroys itself as well. For evil, which lives solely by negation, cannot continue to exist on its own strength alone," Hexagram 23, *I Ching* (Wilhelm, 1968, p. 96).

Other examples of long-term survival can be found in cultures and subcultures that persist in the modern world and which have deep historical roots. Jewish culture (with roots in Judaism) is a striking example. There are just some 14,000,000 or so Jews in the world today. As a people, they have been subject to displacement and diasporas, in which they have found homes in many different parts of the world amongst other cultures. Yet, despite many changing and challenging geopolitical circumstances, they have retained a remarkable unity of culture. Here, I hazard some reasons for this. Although Jews, as a collective, have many political and ideological differences amongst themselves, for example, Zionist and non-Zionist, religious and non-religious, there is a strong collective identity reinforced by traditional practices within families and local communities. Life outside the family tends to be centred on the synagogue, which serves as a place of worship and a community centre. Practising Jews around the world, that is, those who attend the synagogue regularly, keep the Sabbath, celebrate the annual round of religious festivals and engage in the reading of scriptures and singing of psalms according to a prescribed weekly order. There are strong pressures to conform, in some cases, very strong, as found in orthodox communities.[116] In less orthodox communities, it is still common for marriage to someone outside the Jewish community to be frowned upon.

Many other cultures have persisted as part of literate civilisations over many centuries: for example, those based on Christianity, Confucianism and Taoism, Hinduism, Buddhism, and Islam. In all cases, institutions exist - or have existed - to disseminate relevant beliefs and practices and to encourage participation. Often these are subtle and not so subtle forms of oppression. C. S. Peirce states this very clearly in his essay on "The fixation of belief" in his discussion of the fixing of belief by the 'method of authority'.

> Let an institution be created which shall have for its object to keep correct doctrines before the attention of the people, to reiterate them perpetually, and to teach them to the young; having at the same time power to prevent contrary doctrines from being taught, advocated, or expressed. Let all possible causes of a change of mind be removed from men's apprehensions. Let them be kept ignorant, lest they should learn of some

116 In the time of St Paul, the leaders of synagogues had the power to impose a punishment of 40 lashes on those who were convicted of blasphemy. St Paul received this punishment three times for preaching the Gospel of Jesus Christ.

> reason to think otherwise than they do. Let their passions be enlisted, so that they may regard private and unusual opinions with hatred and horror. Then, let all men who reject established belief be terrified into silence. Where ever there is a priesthood – and no religion has been without one – this method has been more or less made use of.
>
> HOOPES, 1991, pp. 152–153

> The method of authority will always govern the mass of mankind; and those who wield the various forms of organised force in the state will never be convinced that dangerous reasoning ought not to be suppressed in some way. If liberty of speech is to be untrammelled from the grosser forms of constraint, then uniformity of opinion will be secured by a moral terrorism to which the respectability of society will give its thorough approval.
>
> HOOPES, op. cit., p. 158

In modern times, Peirce's moral terrorism is known as 'political correctness'.

5 *Opening up Inter-Cultural Conversations*

> Pluralism is a social situation in which people with different ethnicities, worldviews, and moralities live together peacefully and interact with each other amicably … It makes little sense to speak of pluralism if people do not talk with each other – for instance, where people do interact but only as masters and slaves, or where they live in sharply segregated communities and only interact in exclusively economic relations. For pluralism to unleash its full dynamic, there must be sustained conversation, not necessarily between equals, but extended in time and covering a broad range of subjects. Anthropologists have two useful terms for this: commensality and connubium, eating together and/or marrying each other; put differently, we are referring to dinner conversation and/or pillow talk.
>
> BERGER, 2014, p. 1

•••

> It would be foolish to despise tradition. But with our growing self-consciousness and increasing intelligence we must begin to control tradition and assume a critical attitude toward it, if human relations are ever to change for the better. We must try to recognize what in

> our accepted tradition is damaging to our fate and dignity – and shape our lives accordingly.
>
> ALBERT EINSTEIN, https://onbeing.org/blog/albert-einsteins-essay-on-racial-bias-in-1946/ (accessed 30/06/2018)

•••

> The world's greatest – as yet to be tapped – resource is its ethnic diversity.
>
> EDWARD T. HALL, anthropologist

•••

> Star Trek was an attempt to say that humanity will reach maturity and wisdom on the day that it begins not just to tolerate but take a special delight in differences in ideas and differences in life forms. [...].
>
> GENE RODDENBERRY, creator of Star Trek

•••

> My house will be called a house of prayer for all nations.
>
> ISAIAH, 56, 7

∵

Sadly, prejudice and discrimination occur in many forms in many societies. It is often termed 'racism'. This is a misnomer as there is no scientific basis for the concept of 'race'. Unfortunately, many who espouse 'anti-racism' views continue to use the term, giving it a spurious legitimacy. It should be discredited completely. Unsophisticated 'racists' are usually not aware they are speaking in ignorance.[117] There are many other terms in common usage that are not well-

117 I once encountered a 'right-wing' English woman. From her accent and manner, I thought she was a reasonably well-educated middle-class person. I discovered she believed black and white people were different 'species'. I did my best to explain to her that all humans belong to the same species.

defined. They include 'religion', 'right wing/left wing', 'popularist', 'globalist/nationalist', 'multiculturalism', 'black/white'.

Here I wish to make a particular plea regarding the need to open up intercultural conversations. Whilst geopolitics happens at the level of 'statespersons' (waging wars, negotiating peace, making trade deals, arguing over territorial ownership and access to resources) cultural conflicts continue to mar and impede the 'global conversation' (Scott, 2010). Examples are the explicit cultural imperialisms of the Western capitalist democracies, of Islam, of Judaism in the form of Zionism, and other organised belief systems that impose dogmatic creeds by indoctrination and other means. I wonder: how many Jews and Muslims (and, of course, Christians) are familiar enough with the parable of "The Good Samaritan", as found in the Christian New Testament, to be able to tell the story and explain its significance? This short text challenges two often taken for granted concepts, "Who is my 'neighbour'?" and "What does it mean to be 'pure' or 'holy'?"[118]

Multiculturalism (aka 'pluralism'), when it works, usually refers to an unreflexive getting on with each other amongst human beings. In Turkey, for example, many of the Muslim population treat all persons as brothers and sisters, not just fellow Muslims. Troubles happen when demagogues come along and provoke divisions. Irreconcilable differences in beliefs and practices are emphasised instead of being passed over ignored or forgotten. If we are to have cultural melting pots, we need honest and open critiques made with a spirit of love, this is most difficult to implement. A major problem regarding interfaith encounters is the prohibition or active discouragement in some traditions against becoming familiar with the teachings and traditions of other faiths. How do we highlight similarities, differences and distortions, if texts and traditions are not open to scrutiny and discussion?

In contrast to openness to learning about the other (as pursued in many Western schools), there are many ways in which members of particular cultures are dissuaded by their fellows from learning about other cultures. For example, St Paul warns against Christian believers marrying (being 'yoked to') non-believers. In more recent times, the *Islamic Educational, Scientific and Cultural Organisation*, a worldwide organisation,[119] has issued a document with 111 pages, entitled *Strategy for Islamic Cultural Action Outside the Islamic*

118 In Scott (2015), I use concepts from sociocybernetics to analyse what I see as pathological about the Abrahamic faiths.

119 https://www.isesco.org.ma/ (accessed 30/06/2018). ISESCO has 54 Member States, along with three Observer States, out of the 57 Member States of the Organization of Islamic Cooperation https://www.oic-oci.org/home/?lan=en.

World.[120] The text provides guidance about how to preserve and disseminate Islamic culture in host states. There is a warning about "the aspiration of economic globalization to become cultural globalization, imposing a single cultural model worldwide" (p. 11) and "As the danger of 'culture unification' is now threatening Islamic people in their own countries due to the globalization of communication, this danger becomes even more serious when it comes to Muslim immigrant communities and minorities living in a non-Islamic environment, where the new generations of Muslims are raised in institutions not meant for them in the first place." Amongst the many actions advised to counteract culture unification, there is the advice that Muslims should engage in friendly ways with a host nation to further Muslim interests and to take opportunities to proselytise for Islam. However, there is nowhere in the text the suggestion that Muslims should learn about the host culture and its beliefs.

It is a salutary exercise to compare the ISESCO document with a 217-page document produced by the Council of Europe, entitled "*Intercultural Dialogue as a Basis for Peace and Sustainable Development in Europe and its Neighbouring Regions*".[121] Here is an extract.

> The cultural sphere is a domain of the active production, reproduction and renewal of the complex and evolving identities which are themselves the subjects of intercultural dialogue. It provides opportunities for the understanding of increasingly complex identities, often multiple and shared, to be subjected to new perspectives, and for their contradictions to be explored in a non-threatening and often revelatory manner. It engenders new combinations of diverse elements of identity, through fusions and appropriations, which offer exciting innovations. The cohabitation in one locality of different identities has been an important driver of creativity and prosperity, and the recognition of a diversified concept of heritage has become a central component of cultural policy that is relevant to today's changing societies.

Thankfully, there are many who see through the divisions and recognise the universals that apply to the human condition. When I was on a trip to Turkey a few years ago, a young Turkish/Kurdish taxi driver, with little English, engaged me in conversation. He said he wished to improve his English. He went on to say, "No country, no religion, only heart, only human."

---

120 https://www.isesco.org.ma/wp-content/uploads/2015/05/Strategy-for-Islamic-Cultural-Action-outside-the-Islamic-World.pdf (accessed 30/06/2018).

121 https://rm.coe.int/16806b0157 (accessed 30/06/2018).

Part 12 Summing up and What Comes Next

1 *Introduction*

I begin this final part by giving a brief summary of what I have attempted to do in this publication. I also give links to online resources for the reader who wishes to look more deeply into what cybernetics is about and what it can offer. I then give myself the freedom to address the issues we humans face and to make some exhortations about how we should think and act, collectively and wisely. In the final section, I look a little more closely at how, as individuals, we live our lives: our values, attitudes and ethics.

2 *What Next?*

Throughout this publication, I have tried to create and maintain a consistent view of what cybernetics has to offer. It was not brought into being to be a specialist academic discipline. From the beginning, it has offered itself as a way of coming to understand the world and as a way of acting in the world to bring about the futures we desire. My main aim has been to introduce cybernetics to those who are unfamiliar with it. I have also given examples with particular relevance for the social sciences. Not all of these topics will be of interest to all readers. Concerning psychology, I have discussed cognition and consciousness, particularly the ideas of Gordon Pask, which are not well known outside of the UK. I have also used Pask's work in my discussions of the relevance of cybernetics for education. Again, it is fair to say that his work is better known in the UK than in the USA and most other parts of the world, particularly his and his colleagues' studies of styles and strategies of learning, and the design of interactive learning environments. I have also laid stress on his analytical distinction between biomechanical unities (M-Individuals) and psychosocial unities (P-Individuals), which, when applied recursively, provides a richness of forms of explanation for all social levels from a person conversing with herself to the highest levels of collectives. In various parts of the publication, I have addressed communication studies, of relevance for social psychologists, psychotherapists, micro and mesolevel sociologists, and anthropologists. I have only briefly touched on macrolevel sociology, organisational psychology, management science, and design studies. I leave it to the reader with specialist interests to follow up on the references I have provided to learn more about how cybernetics contributes to these disciplinary areas.

For the reader wishing to learn more about cybernetics and the specialist topics that I have briefly alluded to, for example, self-organisation, first and second order cybernetics, autopoiesis, and the biology of cognition, again, I recommend following up on the references I have provided. There are several resources available online that I recommend. Here are a few: Ross Ashby's (1956) *Introduction to Cybernetics* can be found at http://pespmc1.vub.ac.be/books/IntroCyb.pdf;[122] von Foerster's (2003) *Understanding Understanding* is available at https://www.pangaro.com/Heinz-von-Foerster/Heinz_Von_Foerster-Understanding_Understanding.pdf. Four of Pask's books and a selection of his papers can be found at https://www.pangaro.com/pask-pdfs.html; there is an archive covering the work of Maturana and Varela at http://www.enolagaia.com/AT.html; cybernetics related resources can be found at http://pespmc1.vub.ac.be/ and https://www.univie.ac.at/constructivism/. See also the websites of the American Society for Cybernetics (https://asc-cybernetics.org/), the UK's Cybernetics Society (http://www.cybsoc.org/), and the World Organisation of Systems and Cybernetics (http://wosc.co/). A very special source is a paper by Warren McCulloch (1974), "Recollections of the many sources of cybernetics". In places, it is technically challenging but it provides a breathtaking ride through the author's life with an account of the emergence of cybernetics and beyond (available at https://cepa.info/2312).

Alex Riegler, the editor of the journal *Constructivist Foundations*, has created a Constructivist E-Print Archive, CEPA (https://cepa.info/), which contains many texts directly related to cybernetics. It also contains many other texts that follow 'constructivist approaches'. Riegler has identified more than a dozen such approaches that have emerged in recent years (https://cepa.info/approaches).[123] Many, not all, have been influenced by the work of Ernst von Glasersfeld, who, drawing largely on the work of Jean Piaget and the ideas of Giambattista Vico and George Berkeley propagated 'radical constructivism' (von Glasersfeld, 1995). Many years ago, I coined the aphorism, "-isms lead to schisms." As a cybernetician, who looks for transdisciplinary unity, I despair at the many ways in which 'constructivism' is debated. I see this as more noise and redundancy in the academic marketplace. To be fair, there are now authors who look to unify constructivist approaches. An essay in this direction, which I applaud, has been made by Ranulph Glanville, with the title, "Radical constructivism = Second order cybernetics" (Glanville, 2012, available at https://cepa.info/2695).

3 *Exhortations*

> True fellowship must be based on a concern that is universal.
>
> I CHING, Hexagram 13 (Wilhelm, 1968, p. 56)

122 All the links cited in this part were accessed on 19/08/20.

123 For some historical background, see Riegler (2012).

•••

> At any moment we are free to act towards the future we desire.
>
> VON FOERSTER, 2003, p. 206

•••

> There is no true word that is not at the same time a practice. Thus, to speak a true word is to transform the world.
>
> FREIRE, op. cit., p. 68

∴

Although conflict and cooperation are present in the biological world, why is it that we cannot remove conflict from the cultural world? The cultural is distinct. It is the world of human control and communication, human consciousness, human social systems, sociocybernetics. We need to ask, what are the pathologies of control and communication that need to be remedied in politics, economics, legislation, education, social and health care, entertainment, media of communication (mass and social)? Pathologies can be culturally embedded to the point of invisibility. They can be explicitly embedded in rules, laws and other conventions; they are found in the belief systems that people use to give meaning to their lives, that guide their behaviour.

Over millennia, power elites have come into being and taken control; they have reproduced themselves from generation to generation and so it is today; social mobility is largely an illusion. I, myself, have moved from the working classes in England to the middle classes but I am still a million miles away from the established elites.[124] The rich and powerful live in a different world. Access to them is guarded; interaction with them is carefully controlled. Both sides of this divide are lessened by it. Social mobility, at its best, is not about going up or down social hierarchies, it is about having the freedom and opportunity to find one's place in the world, to self-actualise, to discover and use one's talents, to learn how to give as well as receive. Social hierarchies should be temporary things, formed for a useful purpose. The natural human state is one of anarchy, which is what I enjoy most of the time, living as I do in rural

124 In my 20s, I spoke with a young Colombian student about my being from a lower class. She said, "Compared to my country, everyone in England is at the top."

England. Maturana describes this condition well: "A truly human society is.... a non-hierarchical society for which all relations of order are constitutively transitory and circumstantial to the creation of relations that continuously negate the institutionalization of human abuse," Maturana and Varela (1980, Introduction, Point 15).

I write this as we are experiencing the Covid-19 pandemic. Catastrophic ecological disasters are happening now; they will continue and, most likely, get worse, despite our belated attempts to mitigate them. Meanwhile, we continue to have cultural and geopolitical conflicts. Eventually, there are likely to be huge reductions in the global population. The idea of some remnant of human beings escaping to another life-supporting planet is ridiculous. Developments in AI and global control and communications technologies will continue until they are fragmented by shortages of materials, conflict and social collapse. The propaganda wars waged in educational institutions and communications media will continue. We need universal values of caring and sharing, without the burdens of political ideology or religious dogma. Is this too much to ask? We need to nurture a suitably educated subset of the population, with an understanding of the human condition and a desire to work for the good of all mankind.[125] Many with such a desire already exist. However, as yet, they do not speak with one voice.[126] We need the meta-solution of fostering effective solutions. We need to empower and encourage younger generations to be creative and wise.[127]

4 *Values, Attitudes, Ethics*

> It is not the level of wealth in a country that is decisive, but rather commitment to key values, such as the wellbeing of mothers and children, nutrition and education. Without these, no civilization can continue. As long as large numbers of people think they will find their salvation in the faith of scientific technocracy, or any other of these limited faiths, each with its own set of self-supporting but limited and isolating values, modern life will continue to be fragmented, arts and intellectual pursuits will be without a centre of

125 "If anyone wants to be first, he must be last of all and servant of all," Mark 9, 35.

126 The Union of International Associations lists more than a thousand organisations concerned with peace. The list is not exhaustive. See https://uia.org/ybio?name=peace (accessed 17/08/2020).

127 "The superior man acquaints himself with many sayings of antiquity and many deeds of the past, in order to strengthen his character thereby." *I Ching*, Hexagram 26 (Wilhelm, 1968, p. 105).

> gravity, and politics will not be properly related to the real human problems or to continuing human existence in the long run.
>
> BRUCE BUCHANAN (1997, p.714)

∴

When we assign values, we make distinctions and, vice versa, when we make distinctions, we assign values (Spencer-Brown, 1969, p. 1). Buchanan (op. cit.) presents a cybernetic model of value creation and maintenance. For Buchanan, values are metagoals, often tacit, whose attainment and maintenance constrain how other, more instrumental, goals are achieved. For example, one may have the goal of obtaining sustenance but be constrained by the meta-goal of not harming a fellow human being or, in the case of vegetarians, not harming fellow animals.[128]

Von Foerster refers to the ongoing role of values in determining our conduct as our *ethics*. He likens them to a river that underlies all that we do. He cites Wittgenstein (1961, proposition 6.421) in emphasising that it is clear that ethics cannot be articulated. If our ethics do become explicit our use of language degenerates into moralisations, rules with rewards and punishments.[129] "Ethics has nothing to do with punishment and reward in the usual sense of terms ... There must indeed be some kind of ethical reward and punishment, but they must reside in the action itself" (ibid, 6.422). Von Foerster goes on to say, and here I am giving a very terse précis, ethics is not concerned with the truth or what people assert to be the truth (their understandings), it is concerned with the understanding that understandings always rest on the decisions made

128 A note on terminology: many social scientists study 'attitudes': how they are formed and how they may be changed. The concept of an attitude distinguishes the cognitive and affective aspects of values. The cognitive aspect is a statement of belief, for example, "Men are superior to women"; the affective aspect refers to how strongly a particular belief is held and how resistant it is to attempts by others to modify it.

129 The terms, 'morals' and 'ethics', are used in a variety of ways. Sometimes they are used as synonyms. Sometimes ethics is used to refer to explicit rules of conduct and morals is used to refer to personal decisions made in particular situations. On other occasions, as with von Foerster, the usage is the reverse: a distinction is made between explicit moral codes and the ethical choices made in particular situations. A distinction is also sometimes made between 'situational ethics' (as described by von Foerster), referring to personal choices, and 'situated ethics', which refers to the guidelines decided upon by a community with respect to a particular domain of activity, such as medicine, law or other professional practice, buying and selling, parenting, or membership of a club.

about undecidable questions.[130] Von Foerster provides an ethical commitment, "I shall act always so as to increase the number of choices." Von Foerster is inviting us to continue to learn, to be open-minded, to be life-enhancing not life denying. Our languaging, what we say and what we do, makes us aware of ourselves (our 'consciousness'). It also connects us with others and makes us aware of our interdependence (our 'conscience'). Pask (1991) argues that the one fundamental human freedom is the right of actors to interact; he exhorts us to aim for unity without uniformity. Beware of those who restrict that freedom; beware of those who impose uniformity on our ways of thinking, our ways of living and dying, our ways of loving.

Acknowledgements

Many years ago, I suggested to my mentor, Gordon Pask, somewhat whimsically, that cybernetics could well be described as the art and science of fostering goodwill. Gordon accepted the suggestion in all seriousness, reflecting back to me the understanding that I had unwittingly said something of moment. I have continued to study the science and to do my best to practice the art. I have many friends to thank for helping me on my way, too many to list here, but they know who they are.

I give special thanks to my friend, Chaime Marcuello, who first suggested that I write this publication and has done his best, over many months, to keep me on track. I also thank Bernd Hornung, Maurice Yolles and Paul Pangaro who read an earlier version of the publication and made many helpful suggestions for improvement.

References

Abraham, T. (2016). *Rebel Genius: Warren S. McCulloch's Transdisciplinary Life in Science*. Cambridge, MA: MIT Press.

Almaguer-Kalixto, P. and Giglietto, F. (2019). "Steering the world from where we are: an introduction to the sociocybernetics perspective". *Current Sociology*, 67, 4, pp. 479–494.

Almaguer-Kalixto, P., Maass Moreno, M. and Amozurrutia, J. A. (1919). "Sociocybernetics and action research: analysis and intervention in complex social problems". *Current Sociology*, 67, 4, pp. 554–562.

Ashby, W. R. (1956). *Introduction to Cybernetics*. New York: Wiley.

130 For an explanation of the concept of an undecidable question, see part 7.

Ashby, W. R. (1948). *Design for a Brain*, London: Chapman & Hall.

Barabas, A.-L. and Frangos, J. (2014). *Linked: The New Science of Networks,* New York: Basic Books.

Barrett, L. F. (2018). *How Emotions Are Made: The Secret Life of the Brain.* New York: Houghton and Mifflin.

Barsalou, L. W. (2012). *The Human Conceptual System.* In: Spivey M., McRae K. and Joanisse M. (eds.) *The Cambridge Handbook of Psycholinguistics.* New York: Cambridge University Press, pp. 239–258.

Bateson, G. (1972a). "Form, substance and difference". In: *Steps to an Ecology of Mind.* London: Intertext Books, pp. 454–471.

Bateson, G. (1972b). *Steps to an Ecology of Mind.* London: Intertext Books.

Beer, S. (1967). *Decision and Control.* New York: Wiley.

Beer, S. (1972). *The Brain of the Firm.* London: Allen Lane.

Beer, V. and Leonard, A. (2019). *Stafford Beer: The Father of Management Cybernetics: Big Data Analysis Including Cybernetic Glossary.* Independently published.

Berger, P. (2014). *The Many Altars of Modernity: Toward a Paradigm for Religion in a Pluralist Age.* Berlin: De Gruyter.

Berger, P. L. and Huntington, S. P. (eds.) (2002). *Many Globalisations: Cultural Diversity in the Contemporary World.* Oxford: Oxford University press.

Bertalanffy, L. von (1950). "An outline of general systems theory". *British Journal for the Philosophy of Science*, 1, pp. 134–165.

Bertalanffy, L. von (1972). The history and status of general systems theory. In: Klir, G. (ed.) *Trends in General Systems Theory.* New York: Wiley.

Bicchieri, C., Jeffrey, R. and Skyrms, B. (eds.) (1997). *The Dynamics of Norms.* Cambridge: Cambridge University Press.

Birdwhistell, R. (1970). *Kinesics and Context: Essays on Body Motion Communication.* Philadelphia: University of Pennsylvania Press.

Block, J. H. (ed.) (1971). *Mastery Learning: Theory and Practice.* New York: Holt, Rinehart & Winston.

Bloom, B. S. (1961). *A Taxonomy of Educational Objectives.* New York: McKay.

Brier, S. (2008). *Cybersemiotics: Why Information Is Not Enough.* Toronto: University of Toronto Press.

Bruner, J. S. (1960). *The Process of Education.* Harvard: Harvard University Press.

Bruner, J. (1985). "Vygotsky: a historical and conceptual perspective". In: Wertsch, James V. (ed.) *Culture, Communication, and Cognition: Vygotskian Perspectives.* Cambridge: Cambridge University Press.

Buchanan, B. (1997). "Assessing human values". *Kybernetes*, 26, 6/7, pp.703–715.

Buchinger, E. (2012). "Luhmann and the constructivist heritage: A critical reflection". *Constructivist Foundations* 8, 1, pp. 19–28.

Buchinger, E. and Scott, B. (2010). "Comparing conceptions of learning: Pask and Luhmann." *Constructivist Foundations*, 5, 3, pp. 109–120.

Buckley, W. (1967). *Sociology and Modern Systems Theory*. Englewood Cliffs, NJ: Prentice-Hall.

Bush, V. (1945). "As we may think". *Atlantic Monthly*, 176, 1. Reprinted in: Greif, I. (ed.) *Computer-Supported Co-operative Work: A Book of Readings*. San Mateo, CA: Morgan Kaufmann Publishers, 1988.

Cherry, C. (1966). *On Human Communication*, 2nd ed. Cambridge, MA: MIT Press.

Cobley, P. (ed.) (2001). *The Routledge Companion to Semiotics and Linguistics*. New York: Routledge.

Cobley, P. and Jansz, L. (2012). *Introducing Semiotics: A Graphic Guide*. London: Icon Books.

Commoner, C. (1971). *The Closing Circle: Nature, Man, and Technology*. New York: Knopf.

Conway, F. and Siegelman, J. (2006). *Dark Hero of the Information Age: In Search of Norbert Wiener, the Father of Cybernetics*. New York: Basic Books.

Cook, N. and Yanow, D. (2011). "Culture and organizational learning". *Journal of Management Inquiry*, 20, 4, pp. 355–372.

Couffignal, L. (1960). "Essai d'une definition generale de la Cybernetique". *Proceedings of the Second Congress of the International Association for Cybernetics*, Paris: Gauthier-Villars.

Crawford, S. and Ostrom, E. (1995). "A grammar of institutions". *American Political Science Review*, 89, 3, pp. 582–600.

Deacon, T. (1998). *The Symbolic Species*. New York: Norton.

Dewey, J. (1896). "The reflex arc concept in psychology". *Psychological Review* 3, pp. 357–370.

Dorling, D. (2015). *Inequality and the 1%*. New York: Verso.

Durbridge, N. (1994). *Confectionary: Or the Romance of the Word*. PLUM Paper No. 46. Institute of Educational Technology, The Open University, UK.

Ekman, P. (2004). *Emotions Revealed: Understanding Faces and Feelings*. London: W&N.

Einstein, A. (1946). "The Negro Question". *Pageant Magazine*, January issue. Available at https://onbeing.org/blog/albert-einsteins-essay-on-racial-bias-in-1946/#.V4KDRQCSh9k.facebook (accessed 20/09/2017).

Freeman, W. H. (2000). "Brains create macroscopic order from microscopic disorder by neurodynamics in perception". In: Arhem, P., Blomberg, C. and Liljenstrom, H. (eds.) *Disorder Versus Order in Brain Function*. Singapore: World Scientific, pp. 205–220.

Freire, P. (1996). *Pedagogy of the Oppressed*. London: Penguin.

Gagne, R. M., Briggs, L. J., and Wager, W. (1992). *Principles of Instructional Design*. Fort Worth, TX: Harcourt Brace Jovanovich.

George, F. (1961). *The Brain as a Computer*. Oxford: Pergamon Press.

Gergen, K. (1999). *An Invitation to Social Construction*. London: Sage.

Gergen, K., Schrader, S. and Gergen, M. (2009). *Constructing Worlds Together: Interpersonal Communication as Relational Process*. Boston, MA: Pearson Education.

Geyer, F. (1995). "The challenge of sociocybernetics". *Kybernetes*, 24, 4, pp. 6–32.

Glanville, R. (1997). "A (cybernetic) musing: communication – conversation 1". *Cybernetics and Human Knowing*, 4, 1, pp. 59–64.

Glanville, R. (2001). "And he was magic". *Kybernetes*, 30, 5/6, pp. 652–672.

Glanville, R. (2002). "Second order cybernetics". In: *Encyclopaedia of life support systems*. Oxford: EoLSS Publishers. Web publication.

Glanville, R. (2012). "Radical constructivism = second order cybernetics". *Cybernetics and Human Knowing*. 19, 4, pp. 27–42.

Gleick, J. (1988). *Chaos: Making a New Science*. New York: Abacus.

Grice, P. (1975). "Logic and conversation". In: Cole, P. and Morgan, J. L. (eds.) *Syntax and Semantics, Volume 3: Speech Acts*. New York: Academic Press, pp. 41–58.

Gunther, G. (1971). *Life as Polycontexturality*. In: *Collected Works of the Biological Computer Laboratory*, University of Illinois, Urbana, Illinois. Peoria, IL: Illinois Blueprint Corporation.

Gunther, G. (1972). *Cognition and Volition: A Contribution to the Theory of Subjectivity*. In: Collected Works of the Biological Computer Laboratory. University of Illinois, Urbana, Illinois. Peoria, IL: Illinois Blueprint Corporation.

Hacker, P. M. S. (1997). *Wittgenstein on Human Nature*, London: Phoenix.

Hacker, P. M. S. (2012). "The sad and sorry history of consciousness: being among other things a challenge to the consciousness studies community". *Royal Institute of Philosophy, Supplementary Volume 70*. Available at http://info.sjc.ox.ac.uk/scr/hacker/docs/ConsciousnessAChallenge.pdf (accessed 15/09/2017).

Hall, E. T. (1959). *The Silent Language*. New York: Doubleday.

Hall, E. T. (1969). *The Hidden Dimension*. New York: Doubleday.

Harary, F., Norman, R. Z. and Cartwright, D. (1965). *Structural Models: An Introduction to the Theory of Directed Graphs*. New York: Wiley.

Harre, R. and Moghaddam, F. (eds.) (2003). *The Self and Others: Positioning Individuals and Groups in Personal, Political, and Cultural Contexts*. Santa Barbara, CA: Praeger Publishers.

Harri-Augstein, S. and Thomas, L. F. (1991). *Learning Conversations*, London, Routledge.

Heims, S. J. (1991). *Constructing a Social Science for Postwar America: The Cybernetics Group*, 1946–1953. Cambridge MA: MIT Press.

Herman, J. M., Kempen, H. J. G. and van Loon, R. J. P. (1992). "The dialogical self: beyond individualism and rationalism". *American Psychologist*, 47, 1, pp. 23–33.

Hesse, M. B. (1966). *Models and Analogies in Science*. Notre Dame IN: University of Notre Dame Press.

Heylighen, F. (2001). "Bootstrapping knowledge representations: via entailment meshes via semantic nets to learning webs". *Kybernetes*, 30, 5/6, pp. 691–722.

Heylighen, F. and Josslyn, C. (2001). "Cybernetics and second order cybernetics." In: Meyers, R. A. (ed.) *Encyclopedia of Physical Science & Technology* (3rd ed.). New York: Academic Press, pp. 155–169.

Ho, M-W. (1995). "Bioenergetics and the coherence of organisms". *Neuronetwork World*, 5, pp. 733–750.

Holland, J. H. (1975). *Adaptation in Natural and Artificial Systems*. Ann Arbor, MI: University of Michigan Press.

Holland, J. H. (1998). *Emergence: From Chaos to Order*. Oxford: Oxford University Press.

Holland, J. H. (2014). *Complexity: A Very Short Introduction*. Oxford: Oxford University Press.

Hoopes, J. (1991). *Peirce on Signs*. Chapel Hill and London: The University of North Carolina Press.

Hornung, B. R. (2019). "The challenges for sociocybernetics". *Current Sociology Monograph*, 67, 4, pp. 511–526.

Howard, N. (1971). *Paradoxes of Rationality*. Cambridge, MA: MIT Press.

Huntington, S. P. (1997). *The Clash of Civilisations and the Remaking of World Order*, New York: Simon and Schuster.

Jung, C. G. (1916). *Septem Sermones ad Mortuos*. Translated by H. G. Baynes. Reprinted 1967 by Stuart and Watkins, London. The original text is available here: http://gnosis.org/library/7Sermons.htm (accessed 21/07/2017).

Jung, R. (2007). *Experience and Action*. Vienna: edition echoraum.

Kilmer, W., McCulloch, W. S. and Blum, J. (1969). "A model of the vertebrate central command system". *International Journal of Man–Machine Studies*, 1, pp. 279–309.

Klir, G. and Valach, M. (1967). *Cybernetic Modelling*. London: Iliffe Books.

Konorski, J. (1962). "The role of central factors in differentiation". In: Gerard, R. and Duyff, J. (eds.) *Information Processing in the Nervous System*, 3. Amsterdam: Excerpta Medica Foundation, pp. 318–329.

Korzybski, A. (1933). *Science and Sanity: An Introduction to Non-Aristotelian Systems and General Semantics*. New York: The International Non-Aristotelian Library Pub. Co.

Kroeber, A. L. and Kluckhohn, C. (1952). *Culture: A Critical Review of Concepts and Definitions*. Re-published by Pantianos Classics, London: Blackwells (2020).

Laing, R. D., Phillipson, S. and Lee, A. R. (1966). *Interpersonal Perception*, London: Tavistock.

Lakoff, G. and Johnson, M. (1980). *Metaphors We Live By*. Chicago: University of Chicago Press.

Latour, B. (2005). *Reassembling the Social: An Introduction to Actor–Network Theory.* Oxford UP, Oxford.

Lietaer, B., Arnsperger, C. and Brunnhuber, S. (2012). *Money and Sustainability: The Missing Link; A Report from the Club of Rome.* Charmouth, Dorset: Triarchy Press with the Club of Rome.

Lyotard, J.-F. (1984). *The Postmodern Condition: A Report on Knowledge.* Manchester: Manchester University Press.

Luhmann, N. (1989). *Ecological Communication.* Cambridge: Polity Press.

Luhmann, N. (1995). *Social Systems*, Stanford, CA: Stanford University Press.

Maturana, H. (1970). "Neurophysiology of cognition". In: Garvin, P. L. (ed.) *Cognition: A Multiple View.* New York: Spartan Books, pp. 3–24.

Maturana, H. (1995). "Biology of self-consciousness". In: Tratteur, G. (ed.) *Consciousness: Distinction and Reflection.* Napoli: Bibliopolis, pp. 145–175.

Maturana, H. R. and Varela, F. J. (1980). *Autopoiesis and Cognition.* Dordrecht, The Netherlands: D. Reidel.

Maturana, H. and Verden-Zoller, G. (2008). *The Origin of Humanness in the Biology of Love.* Exeter: Imprint Academic.

McCulloch, W. S. (1965). *Embodiments of Mind.* Cambridge, MA: MIT Press.

McCulloch, W. S. (1974). "Recollections of the many sources of cybernetics". *ASC Forum* 6, 2, pp. 5–16.

Mead, G. H. (1934). *Mind, Self and Society.* Morris, C. W. (ed.) New York: Spartan Books.

Miller, G. A. (1956). "The magical number seven, plus or minus two: some limits on our capacity for processing information". *Psychological Review*, 63, pp. 81–97.

Miller, G. A., Galanter, E. and Pribram, K. (1960). *Plans and the Structure of Behaviour.* New York: Holt, Rinehart and Winston.

Mingers, J. (1994). *Self-Producing Systems: Implications and Applications of Autopoiesis.* New York: Springer.

Moreno, J. L. (1934). "Who shall survive? A new approach to the problem of human interrelations". *Nervous and Mental Disease Monograph Series,* 58, pp. 2–20.

Morrison, R. (1999). *The Spirit in the Gene: Humanity's Proud Illusion and the Laws of Nature.* New York: Cornell University Press.

Mulej, M. and Kajzer, S. (1998). "Ethics of Interdependence and the Law of Requisite Holism". In: Rebernick, M. and Mulej, M. (eds.) *Linking Systems Thinking, Innovation, Quality, Entrepreneurship and Environment.* Maribor, Slovenia: The Slovenian Systems Research Society and Partners.

Nelson, T. H. (1990). *Literary Machines*, Version 90.1. New York: Mindful Press.

Newson, J. and Newson, E. (1979). "Intersubjectivity and the transmission of culture". In: Oates, J. (ed.) *Early Cognitive Development.* London: Croom Helm, pp. 281–286.

O'Donnell, P. S. (1919). *Sullied (Natural & Social) Sciences: A Basic Reading Guide.* https://www.academia.edu/9985005/Sullied_Natural_and_Social_Sciences_A_Basic_Reading_Guide (accessed 24/11/2019).

Ormerod, P. (2005). *Why Most Things Fail ... And How to Avoid It.* London: Faber and Faber.

Ouspensky, P. D. (1947). *In Search of the Miraculous.* London: Routledge.

Pangaro, P. (2001). "THOUGHTSTICKER 1986: a personal history of conversation theory in software and its progenitor, Gordon Pask". *Kybernetes*, 30, 5/6, pp. 790–806.

Parsons, T. (1951). *The Social System.* London: Routledge and Kegan Paul.

Pask, G. (1960). "The natural history of networks". In: Yovits, M. C. and Cameron, S. (eds.) *Self-Organising Systems.* London: Pergamon Press, pp. 232–261.

Pask, G. (1961). *An Approach to Cybernetics.* London: Hutchinson.

Pask, G. (1963). "The use of analogy and parable in cybernetics, with emphasis upon analogies for learning and creativity". *Dialectica,* 2/3, pp. 167–202.

Pask, G. (1966). "A cybernetic model for some types of learning and mentation". In: Oestreicher, H. C. and Moore, D. R. (eds.) *Cybernetic Problems in Bionics.* London: Gordon and Breach, pp. 531–585.

Pask, G. (1968). "Man as a system that needs to learn". In: Stewart, D. (ed.) *Automaton Theory and Learning Systems.* London: Academic Press, pp. 137–208.

Pask, G. (1969a). "The meaning of cybernetics in the behavioural sciences". In: Rose, J. (ed.) *Progress of Cybernetics.* Vol. 1. London: Gordon and Breach, pp. 15–45.

Pask, G. (1969b). "The architectural relevance of cybernetics". *Architectural Design*, 7/6, pp. 494–6.

Pask, G. (1975a). *The Cybernetics of Human Learning and Performance.* London: Hutchinson.

Pask, G. (1975b). *Conversation, Cognition and Learning.* Amsterdam: Elsevier.

Pask, G. (1976). *Conversation Theory: Applications in Education and Epistemology.* Amsterdam: Elsevier.

Pask, G. (1979a). "Against conferences: the poverty of reduction in sop-science and pop-systems". In: *Proceedings of the silver anniversary international meeting of the Society for General Systems Research.* Washington: SGSR, pp. xiii–xxv.

Pask, G. (1979b). "A conversation theoretic approach to social systems". In: Geyer, F. and van der Zouwen, J. (eds.) *Sociocybernetics: An Actor Oriented Social Systems Theory.* Amsterdam: Martinus Nijholf, pp. 15–26.

Pask, G. (1981). "Organisational closure of potentially conscious systems". In: Zelany, M. (ed.) *Autopoiesis.* Amsterdam: Elsevier, pp. 265–307.

Pask, G. (1991). "The right of actors to interact: a fundamental human freedom". In: Glanville, R. and de Zeeuw, G. (eds.) *Mutual Uses of Cybernetics and Science (Vol 2), Systemica,* 8, pp. 1–6.

Pask, G. (1996). "Heinz von Foerster's self-organisation, the progenitor of conversation and interaction theories". *Systems Research,* 13, 3, pp. 349–362.

Pask, G. (2011). *The Cybernetics of Self-Organisation, Learning and Evolution (Papers 1960–1972)*. Scott, B. (ed.) Vienna: echoraum.

Pask, G. and Scott, B. (1972). "Learning strategies and individual competence". *Int. J. Man-Machine Studies*, 4, pp. 217–253.

Pask, G. and Scott, B. (1973). "CASTE: a system for exhibiting learning strategies and regulating uncertainty". *Int. J. Man-Machine Studies*, 5, pp. 17–52.

Pask, G., Scott, B. and Kallikourdis, D. (1973). "A theory of conversations and individuals (exemplified by the learning process on CASTE)". *Int. J. Man-Machine Studies*, 5, pp. 443–566.

Pask, G., Kallikourdis, D. and Scott, B. (1975). "The representation of knowables". *Int. J. Man-Machine Studies*, 7, pp. 15–134.

Pentiland, A. (2014). *Social Physics*. London: Scribe.

Pert, C. (1999). *Molecules of Emotion*. New York: Simon and Schuster.

Pessoa, L. (2013). *The Cognitive-Emotional Brain: From Interactions to Integration*. Cambridge, MA: MIT Press.

Piaget, J. (1952). *The Language and Thought of the Child*. London: Routledge and Kegan Paul.

Piaget, J. (1954). *The Construction of Reality in the Child*. New York: Basic Books.

Piaget, J. (1977). *Psychology and Epistemology*. Harmondsworth, Middx.: Penguin.

Piaget, J. and Inhelder, B. (1972). *The Psychology of the Child*. New York: Basic Books.

Pickering, A. (2010). *The Cybernetic Brain: Sketches of Another Future*. Chicago IL: University of Chicago Press.

Pierce, J. R. (1980). *An Introduction to Information Theory: Symbols, Signals and Noise*, 2nd ed. New York: Dover Publications.

Piketty, T. (2015). *The Economics of Inequality*. Cambridge, MA: Harvard University Press.

Poerksen, B. (2003). "At each and every moment, I can decide who I am". *Cybernetics and Human Knowing*, 10, 3–4, pp. 9–26.

Prigogine, I. (1980). *From Being to Becoming*. San Francisco, CA: Freeman.

Ramage, M. and Shipp, K. (2009). *Systems Thinkers*. London: Springer.

Rappaport, R. (1967). *Pigs for the Ancestors*. New Haven: Yale University Press.

Rescher, N. (1973). *Conceptual Idealism*. Oxford: Basil Blackwell,

Rescher, N. (1977). *Methodological Pragmatism*. Oxford: Basil Blackwell.

Riegler A. (2012). "Constructivism". In: L'Abate L. (ed.) *Paradigms in Theory Construction*. New York: Springer, pp. 235–256. Available at https://constructivist.info/riegler/69.

Rocha, L. M. (2001). "Adaptive recommendation and open-ended semiosis". *Kybernetes*, 30, 5/6, pp. 790–806.

Rosenblueth, A., Wiener, N. and Bigelow, J. (1943). "Behavior, purpose and teleology". *Philosophy of Science* 10, 1, pp. 18–24.

Rothbart, M. K. (2012). *Becoming Who We Are: Temperament and Personality in Development*. New York: Guilford Press.

Schrödinger, E. (1944). *What is Life?* Cambridge: Cambridge University Press.

Scott, B. (1976). *Cognitive Representations and their Transformations in the Acquisition of Keyboard Skills*, Ph.D. thesis, Department of Cybernetics, Brunel University.

Scott, B. (1983). "Morality and the cybernetics of moral development". *Int. Cybernetics Newsletter*, 26, pp. 520–530. Reprinted as chapter 5 in Scott (2011a).

Scott, B. (1987). "Human systems, communication and educational psychology". *Educational Psychology in Practice*, 3, 2, pp. 4–15.

Scott, B. (1991). *New Technologies for Open Learning: A Look Ahead*, Unpublished report for the Open Learning Unit, Liverpool John Moores University.

Scott, B. (1993). "Working with Gordon: developing and applying conversation theory (1968–1978)". *Systems Research* 10, 3, pp. 167–182.

Scott, B. (1996). "Second-order cybernetics as cognitive methodology". *Systems Research* 13, 3, pp. 393–406.

Scott, B. (1997). "Inadvertent pathologies of communication in human systems". *Kybernetes* 26,6/7, pp. 824–836.

Scott, B. (2000). "Cybernetic explanation and development". *Kybernetes* 29, 7/8, pp. 966–994.

Scott, B. (2001). "Conversation theory: A dialogic, constructivist approach to educational technology". *Cybernetics & Human Knowing*, 8, 4, pp. 25–46.

Scott, B. (2002a). "Cybernetics and the integration of knowledge". In: *Encyclopaedia of Life Support Systems*. Oxford: EoLSS Publishers, Web publication, https://www.eolss.net/.

Scott, B. (2002b). "Being holistic about global issues: needs and meanings". *J. of Sociocybernetics*, 3, 1, pp. 21–26.

Scott, B. (2004). "Second order cybernetics: An historical introduction". *Kybernetes* 33, 9/10, pp. 1365–1378.

Scott, B. (2006). "Reflexivity revisited: the sociocybernetics of belief, meaning, truth and power". *Kybernetes*, 35, 3–4, pp. 308–316.

Scott, B. (2007). "The co-emergence of parts and wholes in psychological individuation". *Constructivist Foundations* 2, 2/3, pp. 65–71.

Scott, B. (2008). "Observing selves and others: outline of a methodology." *Proceedings of the 19th European Meeting on Cybernetics and Systems Research*, pp. 630–635.

Scott, B. (2009a). "Conversation, individuals and concepts: Some key concepts in Gordon Pask's interaction of actors and conversation theories". *Constructivist Foundations* 4, 3: pp. 151–158.

Scott, B. (2009b). "The role of sociocybernetics in understanding world futures". *Kybernetes*, 38, 6, pp. 867–882.

Scott, B. (2010). "The global conversation and the socio-biology of awareness and consciousness". *J. of Sociocybernetics*, 7, 2, pp. 21–33.

Scott, B. (2011a). *Explorations in second-order cybernetics: Reflections on cybernetics, psychology and education.* Vienna: edition echoraum.

Scott, B. (2011b). "Cognition and language". Chapter 9 in Scott (2011a).

Scott, B. (2011c). "Education for cybernetic enlightenment". *Cybernetics and Human Knowing,* 21,1/2, pp. 199–205.

Scott, B. (2012). "On Reading and Critiquing Luhmann". *Constructivist Foundations* 8(1): 30–32.

Scott, B. (2015). "Minds in chains: a sociocybernetic analysis of the Abrahamic faiths". *J. of Sociocybernetics,* 13, 1. https://papiro.unizar.es/ojs/index.php/rc51-jos/article/view/983 .

Scott, B. (2016). "Cybernetic foundations for Psychology". *Constructivist Foundations,* 11, 3, pp. 509–517.

Scott, B. (2018a). "On messages". *J. of Sociocybernetics,* 15, 1. https://papiro.unizar.es/ojs/index.php/rc51-jos/issue/view/182

Scott, B. (2018b). "Reflections on the sociocybernetics of social networks". In: Lisboa, M. and Cerejo, D. (eds.). *Complexity Sciences: Theoretical and Empirical Approaches to Social Action.* Newcastle upon Tyne, UK: Cambridge Scholars Publishing, pp. 79–87.

Scott, B. (2019a). "On becoming a cybernetician: highlights and milestones". In: Chapman, J. (ed.) *World Futures, special edition, For the Love of Cybernetics,* pp. 101–112.

Scott, B. (2019b). "In defence of pure cybernetics". *Cybernetics and Human Knowing,* 26, 4, pp. 99–109.

Scott, B. and Bansal, A. (2013). "A cybernetic computational model for learning and skill acquisition". *Constructivist Foundations,* 9, 1, pp. 125–136.

Scott, B and Bansal, A. (2014). "Learning about learning: a cybernetic model of skill acquisition". *Kybernetes,* 43, 9/10, pp. 1399–1411.

Scott, B. and Shurville S. (2011). "What is a symbol?" *Kybernetes,* 48, 1/2, pp. 12–22.

Scruton, R. (2015). *Fools, Frauds and Firebrands: Thinkers of the New Left.* London: Bloomsbury Continuum.

Shannon, C. E. and Weaver, W. (1949). *The Mathematical Theory of Communication.* Illinois: University of Illinois Press.

Siemens, G. (2005). "Connectivism: a learning theory for the digital age". *International Journal of Instructional Technology and Distance Learning,* 2, 1, 3–10.

Simon, H. A. (1962). "The architecture of complexity". *Proceedings of the American Philosophical Society,* 106, 6, pp. 467–482.

Sluckin, W. (1954). *Minds and Machines.* Harmondsworth, UK: Penguin Books.

Sørensen, B. and Thellefsen, T. (2009). "Evolution, the true scientist, and his attraction to the highest good: the growth in the concrete reasonableness according to Pearce". *Cybernetics and Human Knowing,* 16, 1–2, pp. 9–26.

Spencer-Brown, G. (1969). *The Laws of Form.* London: Allen and Unwin.

Stiglitz, J. (2013). *The Price of Inequality*. New York: Penguin.

Suppe, F. (1977). "The search for philosophic understanding of scientific theories". In: Suppe, F. (ed.) *The Structure of Scientific Theories* (2nd ed.). Urbana, IL: University of Illinois Press, pp. 3–230.

Thomas, A., Chess, S. and Birch, H. G. (1968). *Temperament and Behaviour Disorders in Children*. New York: New York University Press.

Thornton, P. H., Ocasio, W. and Lounsbury, M. (2012). *The Institutional Logics Perspective*. Oxford: Oxford University Press.

Tomlinson, J. (2012). *Cultural Imperialism*. London: Blackwell.

Umpleby, S. (2003). "Heinz von Foerster and the Mansfield Amendment". *Cybernetics & Human Knowing*, 10, 3/4, pp. 87–190.

Urry, J. (2003). *Global Complexity*. Cambridge: Polity Press.

Varela, F. (1979). *Principles of Biological Autonomy*. New York: Elsevier.

Varela, F. J., Maturana H. R. and Uribe R. (1974). "Autopoiesis: The organization of living systems, its characterization and a model". *Biosystems* 5: 187–196. http://cepa.info/546

Vanderstraeten, R. (2002). "Parsons, Luhmann and the theorem of double contingency". *J. of Classical Sociology*, 2, 1, pp. 77–92.

Von Bertalanffy, L. (1972). "The history and status of General Systems Theory". In *Trends in General Systems Theory*, G. Klir (ed.), New York: Wiley, pp. 21–41.

Von Demarus, E. (1967). "The logical structure of mind (with an introduction by W. S. McCulloch)". In: Thayer, L. O. (ed.) *Communication: Theory and Research*. Springfield, IL: Chas. C. Thomas.

Von Foerster, H. (1960). "On self-organising systems and their environments". In: Yovits, M. C. and Cameron, S. (eds.) *Self-Organising Systems*, London: Pergamon Press, pp. 30–50. Reprinted in Foerster, H. von (2003), pp. 1–19.

Von Foerster, H. (1972). "Responsibilities of competence". *Journal of Cybernetics*, 2, 2, pp. 1–6. Reprinted in Foerster, H. von (2003), pp. 191–198.

Von Foerster, H., (1993). "Ethics and second order cybernetics". *Psychiatria Danubia*, 5, 1–2, pp. 40–46. Reprinted in Foerster, H. von (2003), pp. 287–304.

Von Foerster, H. (2003). *Understanding Understanding: Essays on Cybernetics and Cognition*. Springer, New York.

Von Foerster, H., Mead, M. and Teuber, H. L. (1953). Editors' Introduction to *Cybernetics: Circular Causal and Feedback Mechanisms in Biological and Social Systems*. New York: Josiah Macy, Jr Foundation.

Von Foerster, H. et al (eds.) (1974). *Cybernetics of Cybernetics*. BCL Report 73.38, Biological Computer Laboratory, Dept. of Electrical Engineering, Urbana, Illinois: University of Illinois.

Von Glasersfeld, E. (1995). *Radical Constructivism: A Way of Knowing and Learning*. London: Routledge.

Von Uexküll, J. (2010). *A Foray into the Worlds of Animals and Humans: With a Theory of Meaning*. Translated by Joseph D. O'Neil. Minneapolis: University of Minnesota Press. Originally published in German in 1934.

Vygotsky, L. S. (1962). *Thought and Language*. Cambridge, MA: MIT Press.

Walter, W. Grey (1963). *The Living Brain*. New York: Norton & Co.

Watzlawick, P., Beavin, J. H. and Jackson, D. D. (1967). *Pragmatics of Human Communication*. New York: Norton and Co.

Wells, H. G. (1938). *World Brain*. Garden City, NJ: Doubleday Doran.

Whalley, P. (1995). "Imagining with multimedia". *Brit. J. Educational Technology*, 26, 3, pp. 190–204.

Whitaker, R. (2012). "Luhmann's legacy: illuminating constructivism, or ill-Luhmann-ized constructs?". *Constructivist Foundations*, 8, 1, pp. 32–34.

Wiener, N. (1948). *Cybernetics*. Cambridge, MA: MIT Press.

Wiener, N. (1950). *The Human Use of Human Beings*, Boston, MA: Houghton-Mifflin.

Wilhelm, R. (1968). *I Ching*, translated into English by Cary F. Baynes, third edition. London: Routledge and Kegan Paul.

Wilson, C. and Scott, B. (2017). "Adaptive systems in education: a review and conceptual unification". *International Journal of Information and Learning Technology*, 34, 1, pp. 2–19.

Winch, P. (1958). *The Idea of a Social Science*. London: Routledge and Kegan Paul.

Wittgenstein, L. (1953). *Philosophical Investigations*. Oxford: Basil Blackwell.

Wittgenstein, L. L. (1961). *Tractatus Logico-Philosophicus*. Translated by D. F. Pears and B. F. McGuinness. London: Routledge.

Wolfe, T. (2016). *The Kingdom of Speech*. London: Little, Brown & Co.

Wolpert, L. (2006). *Six Impossible Things Before Breakfast: The Evolutionary Origins of Belief*. London: Faber and Faber.

Wulf, W. (2015). *The Invention of Nature*. London: John Murray.

Yovits, M. and Cameron, S. (eds.) (1960). *Self-Organizing Systems*. London: Pergamon Press.

Ziman, J. (2000). *Real Science: What It Is and What It Means*. Cambridge: Cambridge University Press.

www.ingramcontent.com/pod-product-compliance
Lightning Source LLC
Chambersburg PA
CBHW071351230926
51846CB00002B/503
* 9 7 8 9 0 0 4 4 6 4 3 4 6 *